An Illustrated History of
LIVERPOOL'S
RAILWAYS

By
Paul Anderson

IRWELL
PRESS ≡≡≡

CONTENTS

Acknowledgements

I am indebted to John Ward and Jim Peden of Liverpool - without them this book would not have been possible. Both generously allowed access to their extensive photographic collections, provided information for the captions and supplied vital local knowledge. John Ward also furnished essential details for the maps and undertook meticulous proof reading, the latter reinforced by his wife Patricia. John Gahan kindly allowed me to use part of his book on the Liverpool Overhead and made constructive comments on the resultant text. Peter Binnersley of the Signalling Record Society took the trouble to investigate names and lengths of LNWR tunnels in the city. As usual, I am more than grateful to Allison Bennett for typesetting the maps and photocopying. Juliet Whitworth used her enviable drawing talent to create images of Liverpool to enliven the text.

Front cover, top. The best of Bishop Treacy.

Font cover, bottom. The Pier Head was the focus of local transport in Liverpool. After connecting with ferries from Birkenhead and Seacombe, 1937-built Corporation bogie car No.172 heads up Water Street on 11th September 1955, as an Overhead train for Seaforth rolls into Pier Head station. Photograph B. Mettam.

Back cover. A wonderful aerial view of Garston showing Stalbridge Dock and part of the Old Dock, bottom left. The rows of terraced houses and large factories associated with the port stretch away beyond the quays. Wagons occupy every nook and cranny of the dock area, and there are plenty of fine steam freighters to be seen. Photograph by arrangement John Tatchell.

First Published in the United Kingdom by
IRWELL PRESS 1996
P.O.Box 1260, Caernarfon, Gwynedd, LL55 3ZD
Printed in Huddersfield by The Amadeus Press

Introduction

A prospect looking south from the Royal Liver Building in about 1912. Two Liverpool Overhead trains stand in James Street station near the double bend. The excavation in the foreground of this 'Birdseye View' is the site of George's Dock; Canning Dock is beyond it, and sailing ships occupy Salthouse Dock in the distance. Prominent on the left is the White Star building, whilst the central dome belongs to the Custom House, completely destroyed in the World War II blitz. Construction work on the Anglican cathedral is underway in the distance. Photograph J.F.Ward Collection.

The city of Liverpool is one of that select band of places which have en joyed fame, influence, charisma and sometimes notoriety way beyond their size and apparent stature. This enigma is the result of the enterprise and controversy which have gone hand in hand on Merseyside for well over three centuries. Liverpool's growth began with imports of cotton and tobacco from the New World but accelerated as a result of piracy and slave trading. Massive dock developments brought enormous wealth to the city, yet many of its inhabitants endured appalling squalor in cellar dwellings. Liverpool suffered massive destruction in the Second World War and hundreds of its merchant seamen perished in the Atlantic, but resourceful Merseysiders struggled on and were absolutely vital to the war effort. However, the docks then gained a reputation for strikes and workshy employees, although the inhuman daily hiring of men herded in pens was conveniently ignored by critics. During the 1960s the city took youngsters everywhere by storm with its music, yet intrigues in local politics and social unrest have recently attracted less welcome attention.

Despite its painful eclipse as a port, huge rise in unemployment and numerous other setbacks, Liverpool has pro-

duced a succession of much loved celebrities. It has also retained an earthy sense of humour and warm Scouse welcome for strangers, helped by a lilting nasal accent which is one of the most distinctive in England.

In terms of railways the city had virtually everything - the tremendously significant pioneering route to Manchester, three great passenger termini, a bewildering network of dock branches and sidings, several well known engine sheds, the fa-

mous Edge Hill Gridiron, boat trains with their own quayside station, numerous massive goods depots, suburban stations of every kind, the first deep level urban underground line, and the first overhead electric railway in the world. Although the great liners and cargo ships have gone and the most celebrated ferry in Britain nearly closed down, Merseyside still has a very fine suburban railway system, operated by a forward looking authority. Looking at the built up sprawl of present day Liv-

Bogie car No.777, built in 1933, stands at George's Pier Head on route 22 for Fazakerley in June 1950. St. Nicholas church and the Liverpool Overhead Railway form the backdrop. Photograph G. Shuttleworth.

The Liverpool Railway Network

Scale 0 ¼ ½ ¾ 1   2 miles

N

Maghull

Little Crosby

Thornton

Sefton

Melling

Moor Park

Waddicar

Blundellsands

Great Crosby

Buckley Hill

Netherton

Aintree

Kirkby

Waterloo

Ford

Crosby

Litherland

Racecourse

Seaforth

Orrell

Warbreck

Hartley's Village

Gillmoss

Liverpool Bay

Croxteth

Knowsley

Fazakerley

Docks

BOOTLE

Walton on the Hill

Norris Green

Croxteth Hall

Perch Rock

New Brighton

Knowsley Hall

Docks

Kirkdale

Clubmoor

West Derby

Woolfall Heath

Sandhills

Anfield

Tue Brook

Sandfield Park

Egremont

Newsham Park

Stoneycroft

Little Bongs

Dovecot

Everton

Fairfield

Old Swan

Knotty Ash

Roby

Huyton

River Mersey

Kensington

Botanic Gardens

Broad Green

Page Moss

LIVERPOOL

City Centre

Olive Mount

Court Hey

Bowring Park

Pier Head

Cathedral

Edge Hill

Wavertree

Childwall

Woodside

Cathedral

Toxteth

Gateacre

BelleVale

BIRKENHEAD

Woolton Park

Docks

Princes Park

Sefton Park

Mossley Hill

Calderstones Park

Woolton

Tranmere

Dingle

Calderstones

Rock Ferry

St. Michael's Hamlet

Aigburth

Allerton

Hunt's Cross

Camp Hill

Otterspool

Grassendale

River Mersey

Halewood

Docks

Garston

Garston Rocks

Speke

Airport

Legend

— London & North Western Railway

– – – Lancashire & Yorkshire Railway

••••• Cheshire Lines Committee Railway

✕✕✕✕✕ Mersey Railway

+++++ Liverpool Overhead Railway

—o— Stations

Sandfield   Districts and principal features

▨ Built up area in 1960s

© Paul Anderson 1996

2

JOHN, PAUL, GEORGE & RINGO

...erpool, it is difficult to imagine that this was a remote and underdeveloped corner of England just 350 years ago. Because of the lack of a natural harbour the Romans shunned it, despite establishing nearby Chester as a major settlement on their march north. Walton and Bootle warranted entries in the Domesday Book but there was no mention of Liverpool - although a settlement of sorts did exist in the form of a fishing hamlet clustered around a tidal creek. King John saw some naval potential for the muddy inlet and granted 'Lyverpule' a royal charter in 1207. However, the village languished in obscurity during medieval times, exporting a little Cheshire salt and importing Irish grain, but not sharing the prosperity of east coast ports. It had a small castle overlooking the river (the site is now Derby Square) and the forested Royal Chase of Toxteth, which apparently did not gain much favour for hunting. Inland the red sandstone ridge from Aintree to Dingle was still largely covered with dense forest and beyond it, inhospitable marshland stretched away towards Chat Moss. The estuary itself consisted of shifting channels and shallow banks subject to very high tides which emptied through the narrows at Liverpool with alarming speed.

In 1533 the Elizabethan historian Leland reported that the inlet was 'a good haven with much Irish yarn that Manchester do buy'. A certain amount of expansion was taking place at the time; narrow streets such as Hackins Hey, Quaker's Alley and Leather Lane date from this era as does the fine half-timbered Speke Hall. Liverpool was still an insignificant place during the Civil War and was taken with comparative ease by Prince Rupert in 1644 from his camp at Everton. The defences had always guarded against attacks by sea. However, in the 1660s the harbour began to grow in importance thanks to imports of sugar and spice from the West Indies and Virginian tobacco, a bonus from the colonisation of the New World. Along with other west coast ports such as Bristol and Glasgow, the Mersey was poised to prosper at the expense of towns on the east coast. In 1699, when about seventy vessels entered or left the harbour every day at high tide, Liverpool finally became a separate parish.

The 1700s were an exciting and generally prosperous but controversial time for Merseyside. By 1715 the creek had been converted into a gated wet dock, one of the first in England. But sailing was a hazardous undertaking and many cargoes were plundered by Spanish marauders before they could be landed. Piracy worked both ways however and during the 1740s and 1750s Liverpool thrilled to the exploits of Fortunatus Wright, the scourge of French ships in the Mediterranean. Wright was probably the most famous of the captains whose heavily armed 'privateers' sailed from the Mersey, bringing prizes home. Liverpool itself feared attack from French raiders operating in the Irish Sea and St. Nicholas church on the waterfront was fortified and mounted with guns. South Dock, soon renamed Salthouse Dock because of the increasing exports of salt from Cheshire, opened in 1753 and the magnificent Town Hall was erected the following year.

In the four decades from 1760 Liverpool became one of the most important ports in the world, helped by a vast expansion of the slave trade from Africa to America. Ships sailed from the Mersey to the Niger delta where salt, cloth, iron pots, muskets, knives and brandy were bartered for hapless Ibos collected from the hinterland by local chiefs. By 1764 some ninety Liverpool ships were engaged in the slave trade, many of them using George's Dock which had opened three years previously. The town itself had become a squalid place with rough streets where bullbaiting and cock fighting were rife and harlots preyed on free spending sailors. Wise seamen headed for Mother Redcap's Inn at Seacombe on the Wirral where they took refuge from press gangs and customs officers. The mid 18th century saw Liverpool second only to London in the tonnage handled and justified a stagecoach service to the capital from 1760. The renowned pilot service came into being during 1766, an essential development in view of the eighteen ships which had foundered on the Mersey approaches just two years before.

During the 1770s a disastrous decline in trade with America as a result of the Boston Tea Party blighted Liverpool docks and the number of ships sailing to Africa plummeted from over a hundred to less than a dozen. Sailors rioted, got drunk on plundered wine and even aimed cannon shots at the Liver Bird above the Exchange portico. When the War of Independence ended in 1783 the recovery was remarkable. Trade increased dramatically and the population rose from 35,000 to 60,000 in a decade, although a third were on parish or church relief. Mean dwellings began to cover the erstwhile Toxteth estate but the Liverpool Workhouse (opened in 1771) expanded rapidly as well. Slave traffic burgeoned; from 1783 to 1793 Mersey ships carried 300,000 Africans across the Atlantic. Liverpool Corporation was in favour of this lucrative trade, but there were dissenting voices - notably that of William Roscoe. Eventually the protests succeeded and in 1807 the sad traffic in human cargo was banned from English ships. From 1775 the Leeds & Liverpool canal provided a much needed link with Wigan and around its western terminus 'leafy avenues' were replaced by coal yards. Duke's Dock opened during 1773 followed by King's Dock in 1788, Queen's Dock in 1796 and Manchester Dock in 1806.

Liverpool's population reached 75,000 by 1800. There were large houses for merchants in places such as Aigburth, but well over two thousand people lived in squalid cellars. Some opulent public buildings soon appeared, notably the classical Lyceum Club in Bold Street (1803) and the Georgian Royal Institution in Colquitt Street (1817) which was a pioneering venture in adult education instigated by William Roscoe. The port developed further with the expansion of Duke's Dock in 1811 and the enlargement of Queen's Dock from 1810 to 1816. Scotland Road was laid out as a direct route to the north in 1803. Foundries were established in Tithebarn Street and on the seafront at Dingle (still regularly referred to as the 'cast iron shore') during the early 1800s. The latter produced cast iron fireplaces, door surrounds, window frames and other building components which were used with flair in nearby St. Michael's Hamlet. Iron columns, tracery and other fittings made at the works were employed at pioneering St. George's church in Everton during 1813. More innovation came with the introduction of a steam ferry from Queens Dock to Tranmere in 1817, the famous Birkenhead crossing being converted to steam two years later - although there had been a ferry at this point for some 500 years. As a result numerous Liverpool businessman began to set up home on the Wirral. The early 19th century was certainly not without its spectacular incidents. In 1802 the Goree Piazzas, a row of 1780s warehouses overlooking George's Dock, was ravaged by fire and this burned for three months. During 1819 there was a riot involving Protestants and Catholics.

By 1820 Liverpool was playing an essential role in the industrial development of the north and Midlands, but increasing trade demanded better communications with the hinterland and the next two decades saw the port served by a very advanced transport system. With hundreds of miles of local waggonways oper-

CILLA

ating in many parts of the country, some using primitive steam locomotives, and the ambitious Stockton & Darlington Railway imminent, attention turned to Merseyside. In 1821 merchants from Manchester and Liverpool, unhappy about excessive canal tolls, met to discuss a railway between the two towns. With considerable opposition, all manner of internal wrangling and enormous constructional difficulties, the Liverpool & Manchester Railway gradually took shape. Meanwhile, Prince's Dock opened in 1821. Three years later Jesse Hartley was appointed Liverpool's dock engineer and with seemingly tireless energy went on to build a vast number of quays, basins and warehouses where there had been open shore backed by green fields. His 36 year career also produced a splendid architectural legacy of fortress-like buildings in Scottish granite. Virtually every development in the town had maritime connections. For example, Paddy's Market was established in 1826 primarily to sell second-hand clothing to seamen, whilst during 1829 St. Mary's church at Walton gained a new tower, to help guide ships into the port.

The Liverpool & Manchester Railway opened in 1830 and Britain's true Railway Age began. With the huge success of this line and increasing confidence in the steam engine, all manner of schemes emerged. One of them was the Grand Junction Railway,

promoted in 1832 to link Birmingham (and therefore London) with the Liverpool - Manchester route. At the time Liverpool had a population of over 165,000 and the port was being used by some 11,200 ships a year, bringing trade worth £85 million. Hartley's first docks, Clarence and Waterloo, opened in 1830 and 1834 to cope with the traffic. However, times were still hard and a cholera epidemic swept through the crowded streets during 1833. Lime Street station opened in 1836 at the end of an expensive tunnel from Edge Hill and the first trains from Liverpool to Birmingham used the new Grand Junction line during 1837, connecting services to London beginning in 1838. The Liverpool Fire and Life Insurance Company, the first of many such organisations in the town, was established in 1836 as a result of high premiums for marine risks quoted by London firms. During 1837 the Liverpool Steeplechase was inaugurated at Maghull, moving to Aintree two years later and soon becoming the Grand National. St. George's Hall, now regarded as one of the finest Greco-Roman buildings in Europe, was begun on a site opposite Lime Street station in 1838 but took sixteen years to finish. Brunswick, Victoria and Trafalgar Docks opened in 1836, followed by Toxteth Dock in 1839. The same year saw the completion of the fine classical Custom House near the waterfront.

Railway competition of sorts came with the Chester & Birkenhead line of 1840, and its Monks Ferry terminus (1844) became Merseyside's first riverside passenger station. However, a powerful combine

soon emerged on the Lancashire side. During 1845 the Liverpool & Manchester was absorbed by the Grand Junction and this became a founder member of the London & North Western Railway (LNWR) the following year. The town itself continued to evolve as a place where poverty and civic pride went side by side. The Liverpool Philharmonic Society - one of the first in Europe - was formed in 1840, whilst Prince's Park was bequeathed to the people in 1843, just after England's first municipal park opened, in Birkenhead.

In 1846 an estimated 40,000 people were living in 8,000 infested cellar dwellings, a situation made worse by a mass influx of refugees from Ireland during 1847. Some 300,000 people arrived, crammed on the decks of 'coffin ships' and about a quarter stayed in the port. Many became vagrants and by 1849 over 20,000 children were said to be running wild in the dockland. More emigrants arrived by train en route from Europe or Russia to America and some of these settled in Liverpool as well. A public health officer, the first in the country, was appointed by the corporation in 1846.

Albert Dock, Hartley's masterpiece, opened in 1846 and Collingwood, Salisbury, Nelson, Stanley, Bramley Moore and Wellington Docks followed in 1848-49. The first floating landing stage at George's Pierhead (soon shortened to the now familiar Pier Head) was installed during 1847 and the Leeds & Liverpool Canal was connected to Stanley Dock by a flight of locks in 1848. While all this maritime con-

Railways penetrated almost every corner of the dock estate and millions of tons of freight passed over Mersey Docks & Harbour Board tracks between the 1850s and 1950s. With a large warehouse and street corner pub forming a characteristic backdrop, Avonside 0-6-0ST No.19 of 1924 shunts in Regent Road, Bootle on 30th September 1959. Brocklebank Dock is away to the left. Photograph A. Swain.

The Mersey Railway linked Birkenhead with Liverpool city centre and carried thousands of commuters from the Wirral every working day. James Street station was festooned with advertisements when photographed around 1950. Most were for estate agents, although there was a poster for the Marx Brothers at The Philharmonic Hall and another for wrestling at The Tower, New Brighton.

struction was taking place the long established Liverpool & Manchester/LNWR monopoly in the port was about to be broken. In 1848-49 railways were opened from Southport, Preston and Bury to the northern edge of the town and a new Lancashire & Yorkshire Railway (L&Y) and East Lancashire Railway joint terminus was built at Great Howard Street. At the same time the LNWR opened a branch from Edge Hill to the docks at Waterloo, almost the whole of the steep descent being through tunnels.

During 1850 the L&Y and East Lancashire companies opened an extension to Tithebarn Street in the Exchange area of Liverpool. By now the city's population had reached nearly 260,000 and over 20,000 ships used the port every year, carrying cargo worth £172 million. Sandon Dock opened in 1851 followed by Huskisson in 1852, by which time the need for a railway along the line of the docks had been recognised for at least seven years. Improved access to the quays came with the L&Y Sandhills - North Docks branch of 1855 and after various piecemeal projects a continuous line of north-south rails served the dock estate by 1855. Walton prison welcomed its first inmates in 1855, replacing the old Borough Gaol which had been an obstacle to the L&Y Tithebarn Street extension. In the same year there were hunger riots in Scotland Road as cholera and typhoid swept streets where there was hardly any sanitation.

On a positive note, David Lewis established a modest outfitters shop in Liverpool during 1856 and the Lewis department store empire was born. Half of Britain's imports came through Liverpool by the mid-1850s, but in the first six months of 1857 no less than 337 vessels were held up because of insufficient water or lack of berth space. It was clear that an authority was required to oversee both day to day running and improvements to the port, hence the establishment of the Mersey Docks and Harbours Board (MD&HB) in 1858. Coburg Dock (originally opened as Union Dock in 1816) was expanded in 1858 to deal with palm oil from West Africa, Wapping Dock was completed at the same time and Canada Dock opened in 1860 to cater for increasing timber traffic. The renowned Mersey pilot boats came under the new Board's control during 1859.

Birkenhead docks also came under the auspices of the MD&HB and the town itself came to mirror Liverpool's innovation and growth. From 1860 it had horse-drawn street trams, the first in Britain, whilst through trains to London (Paddington) began the following year. An attempt to reinforce the links between the towns came with the Mersey Pneumatic Railway Act of 1866 which sanctioned a tunnel beneath the river. Several important railway developments benefited Liverpool itself during this decade. In 1864 a LNWR line opened from Edge Hill to Speke on

the former St. Helens Railway (completed to Garston Dock in 1852) and this was a prelude to the shortcut for Euston expresses provided by Runcorn bridge from 1869. The Garston & Liverpool Railway, a modest branch to Brunswick from the St. Helens Railway, opened in 1864. This was destined to become part of the Cheshire Lines Committee system (CLC) which was jointly owned by the Manchester, Sheffield & Lincolnshire Railway (later Great Central), Great Northern Railway and Midland Railway. The CLC was launched in 1865 and soon had a major impact on Liverpool.

An LNWR line from Edge Hill to Canada Dock was completed during 1866, and was known from the outset as the Bootle branch. By this time the Southport line had transformed Bootle from a small village into an important residential settlement with a population of over 6,000, though its short spell as a seaside resort was soon terminated by dock developments. Another line to the quays was the 1867 L&Y North Mersey branch from Aintree and Fazakerley. Concerning the docks themselves, Brocklebank opened in 1862, followed by Herculaneum during 1866. The horrific 'Liverpool Courts' - hovels clustered around fetid yards - were banned in 1864 and St. Martins Cottages, the first council houses in England, were built to replace some of them in 1869. Another sign of the times was the completion of Walton's massive West Derby

Of all Liverpool's local lines, the Overhead Railway was the most distinctive. It was unique in this country - indeed it was less of a surprise to visitors from the USA than those arriving for the first time from other parts of Britain. Train 2-1-9 leaves Brunswick Dock for Seaforth. Photograph J.H. Meredith.

Union workhouse during 1868. For the more affluent the Liverpool Empire opened as an opera house in 1867.

Locomotives began working trains from Edge Hill to Lime Street in 1870; previously stationary engines were employed. The same year saw the inauguration of LNWR passenger services from Edge Hill to Canada Dock and the opening of Wavertree station - the first of several new stations on existing lines to serve Liverpool's growing suburbs. There were major developments for the CLC during this decade. In 1873 the main line from Cressington to Manchester was completed whilst 1874 saw the opening of an extension from Brunswick to Liverpool, mainly in tunnels. A long branch from Hunt's Cross and Halewood to Aintree opened during 1879, the first stage in a bid to obtain more dock traffic for the CLC. There was plenty of business on offer, in 1874 11,548 sailing ships and 7,638 steam vessels entered the Mersey. By this time the population of Birkenhead had reached 52,000 and the Woodside ferry was carrying ten million passengers a year. A railway under the Mersey was therefore becoming an increasingly attractive prospect and trial borings for the 'Pneumatic' tunnel began in 1879. Meanwhile, Liverpool continued to show marked contrasts; Sefton Park opened in 1872 and Wavertree Park, which became famous for its Thursday band concerts, followed in 1879. The Walker Art Gallery, also of 1879, added to the noble group of buildings growing up near St. George's Hall; eventually these included a public library, museum, reading room and technical school. It was a different story on Scotland Road and the waterfront. There were something like two thousand public

houses in the area, with drunkenness, crime, vice and disorder the daily norm.

Liverpool officially became a city in 1880, by which time the population had reached 600,000. The Diocese of Liverpool was formed at the same time and before long plans for a cathedral were formulated. A Royal Charter led to the creation of the university during 1881 and its first building was the magnificent glazed red brick gothic pile by Alfred Waterhouse, which still forms the centrepiece of the campus. Numerous other fine Victorian buildings appeared around the same time, reflecting the fortunes being made from shipping and banking. Yet there were still thousands of barefoot starving children living in hovels or workhouses such as the huge institution on Brownlow Hill near Lime Street station. Attempts to deal with smallpox epidemics and other diseases were reflected in the erection of Park Hill Hospital at Dingle in 1885 and the Fever Hospital in Toxteth during 1888. Council houses were built in considerable quantities from 1885 onwards. Dock developments continued unabated with Alexandra and Langton opening in 1881 and Hornby following during 1884. The railways consolidated and expanded their networks - during 1880 the LNWR reached the nearly completed Alexandra Dock and the CLC opened its line to Huskisson. Passenger services soon followed, but those to the latter was withdrawn as early as 1885. During 1882-83 the famous Gridiron sorting sidings and associated circular goods lines at Edge Hill were brought into use. A CLC extension to Southport materialised in 1884 and quadrupling from Edge Hill to Lime Street was finally accomplished in 1885. The Mersey Railway from Liverpool James

Street to Tranmere in Birkenhead operated its first steam commuter trains during 1886, having previously given up the idea of pneumatic propulsion. Finally, the L&Y Exchange terminus was rebuilt (on a lavish scale) from 1884 to 1888.

Quadrupling of the main line from Speke to Edge Hill was completed in 1891, reflecting the massive amount of traffic which had built up on the southern approaches to Liverpool. During 1892 the Mersey Railway was extended from James Street to an underground station below the CLC terminus at Liverpool Central - again worked by steam traction. Another significant move was the opening of Riverside station near The Pier Head in 1895. This Mersey Docks and Harbour Board terminus soon became the principal transfer point between trains and liners. Access was by way of the Waterloo branch, which had been worked by stationary engines until a few months previously.

The other local line built during the 1890s was wholly different to anything that had appeared before, and had a character all of its own. In fact it became one of the symbols of the city and is still regarded with affection forty years after its demise. The Liverpool Overhead Railway opened in 1893 and 1896, mainly on steel trestles, but including tunnel and surface sections.

Contemporary developments away from the railways were very varied. In 1892 the youthful Everton Football Club opened an impressive stadium at Goodison Park, the first major football ground in England, and newly formed Liverpool FC took over their old pitch at Anfield. Despite strong opposition from the LNWR, L&Y, CLC and Liverpool Corporation, the Manchester Ship Canal opened in 1894. Sprawling Toxteth became part of the city during 1895, whilst Lord Derby presented 22 acres of ornamental gardens to the Borough of Bootle during the same year. A bandstand overlooking the lake provided the focal point for garden parties, where local worthies could forget the relentless clamour of industry and commerce. A School of Tropical Medicine was established at the university during 1898. It has been suggested that this was partly to repay the moral debt of the slave trading years.

Electric traction was the railway theme for the first decade of the twentieth century. In 1900 the Liverpool Overhead began running tramcars from Seaforth to Crosby, then during the following year Walton depot opened to house up to 186 trams for the newly electrified and very extensive corporation street network. The sulphurous and grimy Mersey Railway began running electric trains in 1903, to the relief of regular customers who had not deserted it. A remarkable achievement was the electrification of most local services out of the L&Y Exchange terminus. The Southport line was transformed in

1904 whilst Aintree and Maghull were reached in 1906 and 1909 respectively. Liverpool was experiencing the height of its prosperity and many developments were on a huge scale. Stanley Dock tobacco warehouse was completed in 1900. This fourteen storey building consumed 27 million bricks and was the largest bonded warehouse in the world. The great era of Cunard and White Star liners had begun, with the four-funnelled LUSITANIA reaching New York in less than five days on her maiden voyage during 1907. Prince's landing stage, used by the trans-Atlantic ships, extended nearly half a mile. There was also a maritime tragedy with heavy loss of life in 1909 when the mail steamer ELLEN VANNIN bound from the Isle of Man to Liverpool was engulfed by a wave twenty miles from her destination. The city had a large Welsh element by this time with several Non-Conformist chapels and many streets of terraced houses built with materials and labour from North Wales. It even hosted the National Eisteddfod in 1900. Three years later a competition to design the great Anglican cathedral was won by Giles Gilbert Scott, a 21 year old Roman Catholic. Work began in 1904 and lasted for most of the century.

George's Dock was drained and filled in during 1900 to create a foundation for three huge buildings which have dominated the waterfront for over eighty years. Furthermore, they present the most powerful image of Liverpool and identify the port throughout the world. The MD&HB Dock Office is the southernmost of the

group and opened in 1903. A large central dome, together with smaller ones at each corner dominate this five storey Baroque pile. Beyond Brunswick Street is the Cunard Building, completed in 1914. It is a dour, six storey rectangular block in the Italianate style and was constructed of traditional Portland stone. To the north of Water Street stands the tallest and most distinctive of the trio. The Royal Liver Building - finished in 1909 - was one of the first large reinforced concrete structures in Britain, although stone cladding disguised its skeleton. Two great towers, each surmounted by the mythical Liver Bird with outstretched wings, dominate the ten storey edifice. Also incorporated were the largest clock faces in the country, three on the seaward tower and one facing the city centre. Another massive building, though hardly as prestigious, was the CLC Brunswick goods warehouse which dominated part of the southern docks from the turn of the century. There were even some small scale architectural gems; the famous Philharmonic pub retains its splendid Edwardian interior featuring carved mahogany installed by the same craftsmen who fitted out the great liners.

By 1912 *one seventh* of the world's shipping was registered in Liverpool. Gladstone Graving Dock opened in 1913 and two years earlier the MAURETANIA made the crossing to New York in less than four and a half days. Sadly, deprivation continued in the city; the Liverpool Workhouse had 5,000 occupants in 1910, sometimes sleeping six to a bed, whilst

unemployment and destitution helped fuel riots in 1919, during a police strike. On the railways, L&Y suburban electrification was extended to Ormskirk just before World War I, but Walton on the Hill and St. James (the first station out of Central) lost their passenger services in 1917. During the 1914-18 conflict Liverpool was probably the greatest transport centre at the disposal of the allies for the movement of troops and ammunition.

In 1921 colour light signals were installed on the Overhead Railway and the Mersey Railway was equipped with automatic signalling. However, the most significant transport development of the decade locally was the merger of the LNWR and L&Y, followed almost immediately by the absorption of both systems by the London Midland & Scottish Railway (LMS) which was created at the beginning of 1923. The CLC remained a joint network under LMS and London & North Eastern Railway (LNER) administration. The Seaforth - Crosby trams finished in 1926, but Clubmoor and Warbreck stations opened for residential traffic in 1927 and 1929 respectively. Gladstone Docks were finally completed in 1927, having been delayed because of the war.

By 1930 a quarter of Liverpool's male workforce was unemployed, so the government came up with cash for the Mersey road tunnel in an attempt to ease the hardship. The two mile, £7 million tube was completed in 1934, its huge ventilation towers at Pier Head and Birkenhead adding fresh elements to the waterfront. During 1931, deep in the recession, Mar-

Liverpool's three main line termini dispatched and received trains from virtually every part of Britain. At Exchange in July 1939, Stanier class 5 4-6-0 No.5204 prepares to leave with a Newcastle express.

Liverpool, along with New York, has the most famous waterfront in the world. With the unmistakable Royal Liver Building, Cunard Building and Dock Offices as a backdrop, Liverpool & North Wales Steamship Co. Turbine Steamer ST TUDNO waits at Prince's Stage on 20th June 1956. The 2,300 ton vessel was built on the Clyde in 1926. Photograph W.A.C. Smith.

tins Bank opened its luxurious head office on Water Street. Far less opulent buildings were going up elsewhere, for in the 1930s numerous blocks of council flats replaced once fine houses dating from the city's more prosperous days. Commuting from the Wirral by rail was made much easier by electrification to New Brighton and West Kirby in 1938, through trains of new stock working direct to Central Low Level. Old Roan and West Allerton stations opened in 1933 and 1939 respectively. Mirabel Topham began her long association with Aintree in 1938 - but far off events in Europe during 1939 were destined to change the face of the city for ever.

After the *Luftwaffe* had put the Port of London out of action it turned its attention to Merseyside. Between August 1940 and May 1941 Liverpool was subjected to a terrifying bombardment night after night, the blitz wreaking havoc on the docks and city centre. Half of the large shops in Lord Street were destroyed, the Custom House was reduced to a pile of rubble, St. George's Hall was nearly consumed by fire and the unfinished Anglican cathedral had a lucky escape. The 14th century nave of St. Nicholas church was devastated by bombs but it was subsequently rebuilt to enable this much loved dockside building to continue its role as the parish church. In marked contrast, the shell of the Gothic style nave of St. Luke's church, which was also burnt out, has been retained as a quiet garden forming a lasting reminder of those dark days.

Scores of dock warehouses were gutted, cranes were twisted or toppled and no less than 220 vessels were sunk at the quayside. The most spectacular incident was the explosion of the fully laden ammunition ship MALAKAND in Huskisson Dock. One of its plates was discovered two miles away and a 4 ton anchor was blown over a hundred yards. No.2 branch of Huskisson Dock was devastated and subsequently filled in. Out in the Atlantic the fine modern liner CITY OF BENARES was torpedoed and among the hundreds of victims were some fifty Merseyside children heading for safety in Canada. The railways were badly hit. Huge goods depots such as that at Canada Dock became infernos and the Overhead was broken on numerous occasions, Prince's Dock station never reopening. Exchange approach viaduct was smashed and the terminus was out of action for months. Bootle Strand Road station remained closed for two years whilst the Canada Dock passenger service was permanently withdrawn following enemy action. Nevertheless, the port of Liverpool battled on despite the onslaught and the Admiralty masterminded the Battle of the Atlantic from a bomb-proof operations HQ deep below a city office block. This very secret but utterly vital installation has recently been opened to the public. Furthermore, work essential to the development of the atomic bomb proceeded at the University.

When World War II ended the city was a scarred dishevelled place, but it had sur-

vived and there was a dogged determination to return to normality. Woolworths traded from the basement of its blitzed premises and thousands of tons of debris dumped at Dingle was about to form the basis of a new promenade. This triumphant emergence from the conflict was famously celebrated by Epstein's 'exceedingly bare' sculpture at the corner of a rebuilt department store. Popularly nicknamed 'George' it is a favourite meeting place for all ages. Bessie Braddock, one of Liverpool's most famous MPs was elected in 1945. The railways recovered somewhat less rapidly and the debilitated LMS and LNER (together with the Mersey Railway) became part of the nationalised British Railways (BR) in 1948, although the Overhead remained independent. Passenger trains to Alexandra Dock ceased in the same year, as did the first Corporation tram service. During 1952 the former CLC Aintree - Southport line closed to passengers, Otterspool station shut up shop and electric trains over the North Mersey line through Ford and Linacre Road were withdrawn. The Overhead closed in 1956, the last city tram routes disappeared during 1957 and dingy Wavertree station finished in 1958. More barrack-like blocks of flats were built and sprawling estates created new suburbs. On a brighter note, 1959 saw a competition to design a new Roman Catholic cathedral.

The 1960s was a remarkable decade, even for a city which had experienced so much over the previous three hundred years. Throughout the world the 'Mersey Sound' gripped youngsters and even enthralled their parents, although many would not admit it! It was, of course, instigated by the Beatles - although Cilla Black proved that a Scouse accent suited songs and Gerry and the Pacemakers immortalised the 'Ferry 'cross the Mersey'. This phenomenal wave of talent from Liverpool masked the fact that the city was experiencing a serious decline in its fortunes. The Mersey Docks & Harbour Board was in deep financial trouble despite a £60 million reconstruction of Langton and Canada Docks and the opening of Tranmere Oil Terminal for supertankers. Cunard operated its last scheduled sailing to New York in 1966, evoking memories of scarlet capped porters hurrying from Riverside station to the gangways amid piles of baggage before the Queens of the Atlantic had been challenged by airliners. Endless streets of Victorian terraces in Everton, Toxteth and elsewhere had been demolished and replaced by huge estates such as Halewood, Speke, Belle Vale, Childwall, Cantril Farm and Kirkby. There was a succession of 'last' Grand Nationals and the new 450ft high Beacon appeared in the Corporation's 'City of Change and Challenge' publicity, a telling slogan. There was even a plan to replace Hartley's defiant brickwork and muscular iron columns at Albert Dock with an office block and underground car park.

It was a mixed era on the railways. In 1962 electrification from Lime Street to Crewe was completed, but Central lost its main line trains in 1966. Birkenhead Woodside was the first large Merseyside terminus to be abandoned, closed in 1967. From 1964 to 1969 virtually all local stations lost their goods facilities, whilst several of the once-vast goods depots near the docks closed - although these were already a shadow of their former selves and many had been reduced to open yards by the blitz. The Roman Catholic cathedral was consecrated in 1967 after acquiring the nickname 'Paddy's Wigwam' during construction. Such jibes soon faded away however, for the tapering cone of steel and concrete is punctuated by multi-coloured glass and visitors cannot fail to be captivated by the wonderful light effects inside. Bessie Braddock retired from politics in 1969 but Harold Wilson, MP for Huyton and once and future Prime Minister - ensured that Liverpool still had a strong representative in Westminster.

Railway retrenchment continued with the closure of Riverside in 1971. The former CLC terminus at Central and associated local stations as far as Garston were abandoned when the local service to Gateacre was withdrawn during 1972. Crown Street goods, a survivor from pioneering Liverpool & Manchester days, perished in the same year. Royal Seaforth Docks, a massive development of 85 acres, opened in 1973 specifically for container traffic and bulk cargoes but was without rail access at first. During 1974 the second Mersey road tunnel was completed and it was announced that the loss making ferries would probably finish in about two years. With industrial disputes plaguing the port, the MD&HB finally went bankrupt with debts of £90 million. Liverpool's population had decreased by 200,000 since the war (a great many moving to new towns at Skelmersdale, Runcorn and Winsford), a more rapid decline than in any other British city. Huge office blocks and hotels were rearing up in the city centre and close by The Pier Head but the situation elsewhere was depressing. In 1970 no less than 63 families occupied just eleven houses in one Toxteth street and near the University new council blocks replacing slums which had once been the abode of the well to do soon became run-down themselves. Perhaps the mid-1970s will prove the low point in the city's fortunes.

In 1974 Aintree racecourse was acquired by a Liverpool property developer who was determined that the old pageantry would return - Red Rum saw that it did. The great Anglican cathedral built in the Gothic style from locally quarried red sandstone, was finally completed in 1978. The 347 feet tower which dominates the largest Anglican church in the world is visible from a great distance. This monumental building and the equally striking Roman Catholic cathedral are appropriately situated at the opposite ends of Hope Street. Merseyside Passenger Transport Executive was created in 1974 to look after trains and buses in the new Metropolitan county. It nurtured a bold project already underway, and soon began developing the rail network further. The Cavern Club, where the Beatles began their career, was sacrificed during 1973 for excavations associated with the Liverpool Loop, which was to bring Wirral trains via the Mersey tunnel round an underground circle beneath the city centre. In 1977 construction work was completed and stations at Moorfields, Lime Street and Central akin to those on the London tube, opened to the public. At the same time the once-grand L&Y terminus at Exchange was closed and trains from Southport, Ormskirk and Kirkby made their way to Central Low Level along a new underground alignment. These Northern Line electric services were extended from Central to Garston using the previously derelict ex-CLC route in 1978.

The Merseyside Development Corporation was formed in 1981 with substantial financial backing to help revitalise Liverpool and Birkenhead, a daunting task. Frustration in the inner suburbs boiled over that summer when Toxteth erupted in several nights of rioting, looting and burning, although to be fair, the chaos in Liverpool 8 also took place elsewhere in England. A symbol of the brave new world was the first International Garden Festival (complete with a fine two foot gauge railway) near the site of Herculaneum Dock during 1984, and the charisma of the city was clearly reflected on television. *Brookside* became one of the most popular 'soaps' and earlier on, *The Liver Birds* used one of the many rhymes associated with back street skipping games as its signature tune. Despite declining maritime activity, seventeen docks remained active in 1988 and sense prevailed when Albert Dock opened as a smart shopping arcade and maritime museum during 1989. It also incorporated the Northern Tate Gallery, reflecting the city's growing role as a centre for tourism and the arts. Even the reprieved ferry to Woodside and Seacombe is now being promoted as an attraction in its own right. Although rather a shadow of their former selves, the railways still serve Liverpool well in the 1990s. There is a 15 minute off-peak service on most local lines and the distinctive yellow, grey, black and white Merseytravel electrics are well maintained. A very cheap scratch card allows freedom of the system outside the rush hours. Goods traffic from the docks is now confined to the freightliners and coal trains out of Seaforth, but even these provide interest as they weave their way through the recesses of Bootle.

A ferry journey from Woodside to The Pier Head at dusk is a memorable experience, especially for the first time. The Royal Liver, Cunard and Dock Office buildings, now cleaned up and beautifully illuminated, gradually grow in stature as the diesel engine throbs below deck and a cool breeze comes in from the Irish Sea. This is as good a place as any to contemplate the past, present and future of Merseyside. Liverpool is unique, for the city has the individuality of Glasgow, and probably more in common with Dublin than other urban areas in England. Let the imagination wander back to the days when Maggie May and other 'judies' sauntered along Lime Street, and Paradise Street inspired sea shanties such as 'Blow the Man Down'. In more recent times the Scaffold even celebrated a railway marshalling yard by singing 'Thank U Very Much for the Aintree Iron'! Glance seawards and imagine a Canadian Pacific, Cunard or Elder Dempster liner setting off for the United States. Look shorewards again and take in the scene no doubt proudly viewed by so many famous sons of the city - Tommy Handley, Arthur Askey, Ted Ray, Ken Dodd, Jimmy Tarbuck, The Beatles and John Conteh, to name but a few. This book aims to celebrate in words and pictures just one aspect of this remarkable place - the railways which were so vital to its commercial growth.

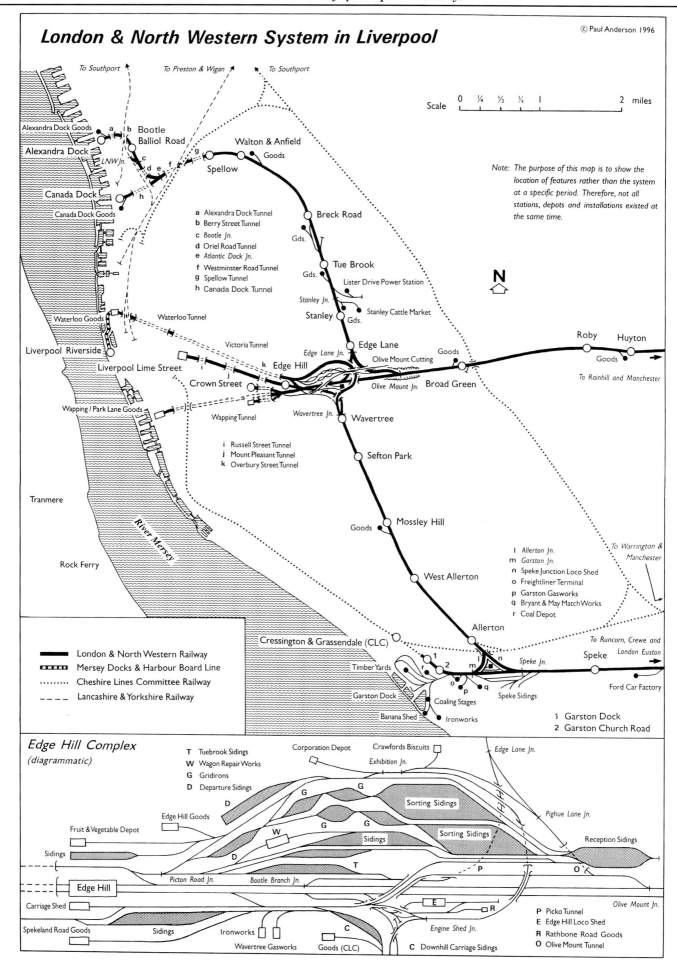

London & North Western System in Liverpool

© Paul Anderson 1996

Scale 0 ¼ ½ ¾ 1 2 miles

Note: The purpose of this map is to show the location of features rather than the system at a specific period. Therefore, not all stations, depots and installations existed at the same time.

To Southport
To Preston & Wigan
To Southport

Alexandra Dock Goods
Bootle Balliol Road
Walton & Anfield
Goods
Alexandra Dock
LNW Jn.
Spellow
Canada Dock
Canada Dock Goods

a Alexandra Dock Tunnel
b Berry Street Tunnel
c *Bootle Jn.*
d Oriel Road Tunnel
e *Atlantic Dock Jn.*
f Westminster Road Tunnel
g Spellow Tunnel
h Canada Dock Tunnel

Breck Road
Gds.
Tue Brook
Gds.
Lister Drive Power Station
Stanley Jn.
Stanley
Stanley Cattle Market
Gds.
Edge Lane
Olive Mount Cutting
Edge Lane Jn.
Goods

Roby   Huyton
Goods

N

To Rainhill and Manchester

Waterloo Goods
Waterloo Tunnel
Liverpool Riverside
Victoria Tunnel
Liverpool Lime Street
k Edge Hill
Crown Street
Olive Mount Jn.   Broad Green
Wapping / Park Lane Goods
Wapping Tunnel
Wavertree Jn.   Wavertree

Tranmere

i Russell Street Tunnel
j Mount Pleasant Tunnel
k Overbury Street Tunnel

Sefton Park

River Mersey

Rock Ferry

Mossley Hill
Goods

To Warrington & Manchester

l Allerton Jn.
m Garston Jn.
n Speke Junction Loco Shed
o Freightliner Terminal
p Garston Gasworks
q Bryant & May Match Works
r Coal Depot

West Allerton

Allerton

Cressington & Grassendale (CLC)

To Runcorn, Crewe and London Euston

Speke

Timber Yards
Garston Dock
Banana Shed
Ironworks
Coaling Stages
Speke Sidings
Speke Jn.
Ford Car Factory

1 Garston Dock
2 Garston Church Road

Legend:
— London & North Western Railway
▭ Mersey Docks & Harbour Board Line
⋯ Cheshire Lines Committee Railway
- - - Lancashire & Yorkshire Railway

Edge Hill Complex
(diagrammatic)

T Tuebrook Sidings
W Wagon Repair Works
G Gridirons
D Departure Sidings

Corporation Depot
Crawfords Biscuits
Exhibition Jn.
Edge Lane Jn.

Edge Hill Goods
Fruit & Vegetable Depot
Sidings
W
G   G
Sidings
Sorting Sidings
Sorting Sidings
Pighue Lane Jn.
Reception Sidings
D
T
P
O

Edge Hill
Picton Road Jn.   *Bootle Branch Jn.*

Carriage Shed
Spekeland Road Goods
Sidings
Ironworks
Wavertree Gasworks
Goods (CLC)
C
E
R
Engine Shed Jn.
Olive Mount Jn.

P Picko Tunnel
E Edge Hill Loco Shed
R Rathbone Road Goods
O Olive Mount Tunnel
C Downhill Carriage Sidings

Chapter 1

NORTH WESTERN

The magnificent yet somewhat cluttered frontage of Lime Street station, on 11th September 1955. Part of the huge and unashamedly ornate North Western Hotel is visible on the left. The smaller Royal Hotel on the right was built when the terminus was in its infancy. Streamlined bogie car No 951, dating from 1937, heads south along Lime Street. Photograph B. Mettam.

London & North Western tracks formed the backbone of Liverpool's railway system and most of this network is still open. It includes the main line from Lime Street to Crewe (the first part of the West coast route to be electrified) and the last surviving line into the

MP FOR HUYTON

docks. The celebrated Liverpool & Manchester Railway through Huyton, Roby and Edge Hill to Crown Street and Wapping was the first element in this pattern and it soon spawned branches to Lime Street passenger terminus in the middle of the city and Waterloo goods depot, near the busiest docks. Improved access to the south, the present main line, came with a connection between Speke and Edge Hill which sprang from an earlier branch from Warrington to Garston Dock. As the port spread northwards, a line was built through Tue Brook and Walton to Canada Dock and Alexandra Dock; it was always a vital freight artery

but passenger trains, ranging from Southport-Euston through coaches to Grand National specials, used it as well. Edge Hill developed into an immensely complex railway centre incorporating a bewildering array of goods lines, the famous 'gridiron' marshalling yards and one of Britain's best known engine sheds. With both the railways and trans-Atlantic liners approaching their zenith, Riverside station was opened just beyond Waterloo

goods depot. Inevitably, there has been some retrenchment. Riverside, Crown Street and Alexandra Dock stations have been obliterated, together with the 'gridiron' and Edge Hill shed. However, the Liverpool & Manchester approach through Olive Mount cutting and Edge Hill is as impressive as ever, and Lime Street terminus has improved over the last few years.

Crown Street tunnel, looking towards Edge Hill, on 11th August 1957. The superb stonework had clearly been cut back at some time to accommodate larger wagons. On the left, a plaque reads 'This tunnel constructed in 1829 by George Stephenson served the original passenger terminus of the Liverpool and Manchester Railway at Crown Street'. Passenger services ceased in 1836 on the opening of Lime Street station, but goods traffic continued until 1972. Photograph C.A. Appleton.

The western portal of Wapping tunnel, looking towards Edge Hill in the 1930s. Built in 1826-29, it was almost 2,000 yards long and had a ruling gradient of 1 in 48. Cable haulage uphill and gravity with brake vans downhill lasted until 1896, and locomotives then served until closure in 1965. The wooden flooring was presumably to assist horses. Other interesting features include the complicated pointwork starting in the tunnel, several capstans, and a remarkably slim signal cabin. The significance of the whitewashed archway is not known. Photograph D. Ibbotson.

LIVERPOOL & MANCHESTER

In a September 1914 *Railway Magazine* article, Basil Mercer stated *'To everyone interested in the history of railways in England the name of the Liverpool and Manchester is as familiar as the appearance of a taxicab in London ... but as a matter of fact it is one of those lines which many have heard about and few know anything of'*. Since then plenty has been written about this immensely important railway and a tremendous amount of interest was generated in 1980 by the cavalcade at Rainhill, celebrating its 150th anniversary. But a history of Liverpool's railways would be incomplete without an outline of the genesis, construction and operation of what has often been called the world's first proper railway.

The population of both Liverpool and Manchester more than doubled from 1791 to 1821. In the same period the number of cotton bags unloaded at Liverpool increased from 400 to 400,000 and power looms at work in the Manchester area reached 30,000. Furthermore, Lancashire-built machinery was being exported to America in vast quantities. Three canals, together with the turnpike road, competed for this traffic, but the fastest transit time between the two centres was no less than 36 hours. William James, an enterprising land agent with civil engineering and colliery interests, came to Liverpool in 1822, having studied steam locomotives at work on colliery tramways. He was adamant that such machines could be employed for passenger and general goods traffic over longer distances. After surveying the ground in the face of considerable resistance, he proposed a 31 mile railway between Lancashire's principal towns, via Huyton, Rainhill, Newton and Eccles. Although failing health precluded James

from carrying out further work, his idea took root and a committee was formed. George Stephenson was engaged because of his experience with the Stockton & Darlington Railway, and he suggested a more northerly course via Walton, Fazakerley, Kirkby, Knowsley, Leigh and Eccles. Opposition from canal proprietors was understandable, but ordinary members of the public, frightened of change, were hostile as well and the scheme was rejected by the House of Commons in 1825. Stephenson was dismissed, George and John Rennie were appointed engineers, and Charles Vignoles was asked to

survey the original alignment again. This time parliament was convinced and it is no exaggeration to say that one of the great milestones in the history of the world occurred on 5th May 1826, when the railway from Wapping to Salford received the Assent.

There were still huge problems ahead - most of them involved engineering difficulties, although disagreements in the Liverpool & Manchester boardroom did not help. The Rennies were invited to supervise construction with George Stephenson as resident engineer, but George Rennie was unhappy about this arrangement and promptly resigned. Stephenson was reappointed in July 1926 and proved a wise choice. He understood the overall concept of the line, had the necessary drive to overcome opposition, and was a great manager of the workforce. Construction began in summer 1826 and gradually the famous engineering achievements at Wapping tunnel, Olive Mount cutting, Chat Moss and Sankey viaduct took shape. Although as late as 1828 several experts still advocated the use of stationary engines, the Liverpool & Manchester management embraced the vision of William James and arranged a competition for steam locomotives a year before the line opened. The Rainhill Trials of 6th October 1829 will always be regarded as one of the great occasions in the history of railways and even the casual reader will probably know that Stephenson's ROCKET outclassed the opposition.

In bright sunshine on 15th September 1830 the Liverpool & Manchester Railway was opened by the Duke of Wellington during a glittering ceremony watched by a huge and excited crowd. The day ended

The cotton quay at Park Lane undergoing repairs, probably as a result of wartime damage, on 24th September 1953. This was just a small part of the huge Wapping complex, first established by the Liverpool & Manchester Railway.

A former Lancashire & Yorkshire 0-4-4T in use as a stationary boiler at Edge Hill carriage shed, close to Tunnel Road, on 13th June 1964. Four of the six-wheel brake vans used in Wapping tunnel (Nos M732316/18/13/14) stand beyond it. Tracks in the foreground led to Wapping and Crown Street goods stations. Photograph J.F. Ward.

with heavy rain, a number of minor accidents and the death of Liverpool MP William Huskisson who fell beneath the wheels of ROCKET. This unfortunate incident did not detract from the significance of the occasion. Liverpool had promoted and financed a scheme which was described at the time as the 'Grand British Experimental Railway'. It brought several significant elements together - a public line authorised by Act of Parliament; steam traction in general and recognisable stations. Regular passenger services began on 17th September 1830, but normal goods traffic was delayed for a few weeks because of locomotive shortage and incomplete facilities at intermediate stations.

and slightly curved for some 270 yards, but dead straight and inclined at 1 in 48 for the remainder of its passage. The double track tunnel, 22 feet wide and 16 feet high, was whitewashed and gas lit at first, an extravagance of those pioneering days. Although longer and more complex canal tunnels had been built years before, the Liverpool work was still hailed as a masterpiece. Wapping depot stood in a cutting, so the goods sheds and warehouses were built above the tracks just west of the tunnel mouth. In LNWR days the site was more than doubled in size and enclosed by a huge perimeter wall with mas-

sive gates. From 1844 lines extended beyond the yard across a swingbridge to King's Dock.

Crown Street passenger terminus was virtually above Wapping tunnel, about 350 yards from its eastern portal. A second tunnel, 291 yards long provided access, but it was a mere 15 feet wide by 12 feet high - clearly not intended for locomotives. Crown Street station was remarkable for its time, a purpose built terminus which established the basic pattern for such structures. It consisted of an austere but nevertheless homely two storey classical building with large plain windows and doorways. The solitary low platform was sheltered by a flat canopy supported on slender iron columns at the outer edge. A gabled timber train shed extended across three tracks to a screen wall opposite. Waiting rooms and a ticket office were provided, normal features of thousands of subsequent stations but an innovation here. Crown Street was not used for regular services until December 1830 and it soon proved inconvenient - not for its facilities, but because of its location, amid uncompleted streets over a mile from Lime Street. At least first class passengers had the luxury of horse drawn carriages to the centre of Liverpool.

Crown Street and Wapping tunnels emerged at Edge Hill in a 40 feet deep excavation known, somewhat confusingly, as Wapping cutting. In the early days this was a remarkable site, both architecturally and in terms of activity. The most extraordinary feature was the famous Moorish Arch (so called because of its Turkish style) linking twin towers housing winding engines. These operated cables which hauled wagons out of Wapping goods yard and passenger car-

An impression of Crown Street station. Drawing by Juliet Whitworth.

Access to the docks at Liverpool was a prime consideration. Stephenson's original route would have come in from the north, avoiding the sandstone ridge from Aintree to Dingle, but the adopted course had to tackle this obstruction. Surface running through the streets was ruled out by the Corporation, so a tunnel was inevitable. Wapping goods station stood about 25 feet above sea level and the climb to approximately 150 feet at Edge Hill was accomplished in a 2,240 yard bore, level

Broadgreen station, looking east on 21st July 1968, shortly before the two right hand fast lines and all the buildings were removed to make way for an M62 link road. The two remaining platforms still handle a considerable amount of local passenger traffic. Photograph J.F. Ward.

Roby station, looking east on 15th August 1971. The former slow lines on the left were being lifted. Huyton signal box and station are just visible in the distance. Photograph J.F. Ward.

Huyton station, looking east on 15th August 1971. Like Broadgreen and Roby, this was one of the original Liverpool & Manchester stopping places. The only remaining tracks are those in the foreground. Buildings to the left have been demolished, but the semaphore signals still survived in 1996. Photograph J.F. Ward.

engineering achievements. Beyond a fairly featureless area around Edge Hill the sandstone rose again at Olive Mount and almost half a million cubic yards of rock was removed to create a chasm-like excavation nearly 80 feet deep, just 20 feet wide and over half a mile long. Olive Mount cutting was regarded with awe and wonder at the time, and even when it was widened in 1870-71 to accommodate quadruple track, the overall effect was scarcely less impressive. Further east the ground fell away steadily and material from the cutting was used to create Roby embankment, two miles long and up to 45 feet high. There was much favourable comment about the views it afforded of nurseries, woodland and country houses. On this section three stopping places were provided where the line crossed roads, namely Broad Green, Roby Gate and Huyton Gate. These early halts were all established by the time the February 1831 timetable was issued and they remain as present day stations, more or less on their original sites.

Initially there were six trains each way between Liverpool and Manchester, the journey time being about two hours and the maximum speed 30mph. Success was instant, with some 70,000 passengers travelling on the railway by the end of 1830. Despite its bold concept and execution, the line literally creaked under pressure as a result of its popularity. By 1834 both passenger and goods traffic was flowing between Liverpool and St Helens, Warrington, Wigan, Leigh and Bolton over various connections. The original wrought iron rails proved far too light and were replaced after six years, whilst Crown Street passenger station was doomed in 1832 when the branch to Lime Street was authorised. This important extension opened in 1836 and is the subject of the next section. By 1837 there were ten passenger trains a day each way and the jour-

riages up the slight rise to Crown Street. Above the tunnel mouth were two 100 feet high chimneys in the form of enormous Ionic columns which were furnace flues for the winding engine boilers. Deep alcoves in the rock face accommodated locomotives, the first recorded engine sheds in the world. During the early 1830s this 'Grand Area at Edge Hill' would have seen wagons being transferred to and from Wapping incline, passenger carriages making their way into and out of Crown Street, and engines being serviced and turned. Nearby was Wavertree Lane station, the terminus until Crown Street became fully operational in December 1830 but closed in August 1836, shortly after Edge Hill opened.

After a brief level stretch at Edge Hill, the Liverpool & Manchester descended at 1 in 1092 for just over five miles. This almost imperceptible gradient was only maintained, however, by two impressive

A dark corner of Lime Street (complete with ghostly legs) on 8th March 1950, looking down the length of platform 1. The station furniture and signs were still very much LNWR.

Part of the concourse at Lime Street on 8th March 1950. Wymans bookstall and the Empire tobacco and refreshments kiosk are doing well. They were brand new, the original having been demolished by a runaway train four months previously! The cab road is still cobbled. Among the numerous advertisements are those for BMK Mothproof carpets and rugs, Duraflex shoes (their comfort costs you nothing) and National Accounting Machines (speed the working day).

ney was down to 1 hour 15 minutes. Somewhat remarkably, the Liverpool & Manchester Railway enjoyed a monopoly in England's second port for nearly twenty years despite several rival schemes. The Railway Mania of 1844-5 led to an eruption of threatening proposals, and the Grand Junction Railway (opened from Birmingham Vauxhall to Earlestown on the Liverpool & Manchester in 1837) was deeply concerned about comfortable access to Merseyside. By mutual consent it took over the old pioneer on 8th August 1845 and in turn became a founder member of the London & North Western Railway, on 1st January 1846.

With the Railway Age gaining momentum, the western end of the Liverpool & Manchester experienced considerable changes. In 1849 the LNWR opened a cable operated incline from Edge Hill down to the docks at Waterloo (see later) and the new winding engine also dealt with traffic from Wapping. The original winding houses in Wapping cutting, together with the Moorish Arch, were then demolished. At the same time a blind tunnel immediately south of those to Crown Street and Wapping, previously used as a workshop, was extended for a hundred yards or so to provide an alternative access to Crown Street. Passenger services had been withdrawn from the original terminus on 15th August 1836 when Lime Street opened, and the site became a coal depot with sidings eventually extending south to Falkner Street, west to Olive Street, and north to a large yard between Crown Street and Smithdown Lane.

Meanwhile, the main line was going from strength to strength with non-stop trains to Manchester taking just 45 minutes from 1859. The Liverpool end of the route gained three feeder lines in rapid succession - Edge Hill to Speke (1864), Edge Hill to Canada Dock (1866) and Huyton to St Helens (1871). Locomotives replaced cable operation on the Wapping branch in 1896. By that time Edge Hill had become an immense and complex railway centre, and is dealt with in the last section.

The significance of the Liverpool & Manchester railway was emphasised by celebrations marking its centenary in 1930, when there was still plenty to see at the western extremity. But declining goods traffic brought considerable changes thirty to forty years later. Wapping depot, which had been known as Park Lane since 1923, was closed on 1st November 1965 and gradually demolished. The site became an industrial estate ten years later. Crown Street goods finished on 1st May 1972, the surviving part of the Liverpool & Manchester passenger station having

The opulent interior of the North Western Hotel could even be experienced by transient passengers visiting Lime Street station buffet. Huge columns, partly fluted and terminating in ornate capitals, supported the ceiling, which was panelled and finished off with decorative plaster work. Garlands and festoons adorned the end walls. At 10.30am on 16th June 1953 the customers did not seem particularly overawed by the surroundings; in fact the chap on the left looked quite depressed!

15

Looking towards the departure end of Lime Street on 2nd January 1957. The main line stock was in the transitional stage between 'blood and custard' and lined maroon livery.

last quarter of a mile being 1 in 83, and a terminus opposite St Georges Hall, then in the planning stage. Liverpool Corporation's attitude to the new line was confusing. On the one hand it had a clause inserted in the Bill prohibiting locomotives from entering the city, so another winding engine was installed at Edge Hill to work trains up and down the incline by cable. At the same time it obviously welcomed the extension and subscribed £2,000 to embellish the station facade. Passenger trains from Manchester were diverted to Lime Street on 15th August 1836.

Like Crown Street, the original station at Lime Street was a pioneering venture and established the basic pattern employed for other important termini over the next few years. It had two side platforms - one for arrivals and one for departures - with carriage sidings in the middle. The most innovative feature was a large overall roof spanning the platform area almost up to the tunnel portal. Designed by George Stephenson, it was the

been burnt out during the blitz. The site is now a car park. Huyton good yard closed on 1st March 1965, but Broad Green remained open to deal with W H Smith private sidings traffic. The 150th anniversary celebrations in 1980 included a spectacular recreation of the Rainhill Trials and a trail was opened in Wapping cutting to permit access to the remaining features at this historic location. In 1996 the Liverpool & Manchester line between Edge Hill and Huyton had about eighty passenger services each way, mostly stopping trains and just over half of them Merseytravel locals to and from St Helens Central. The Lime Street-Manchester Victoria expresses were still flourishing however, the fastest taking 48 minutes including four intermediate stops. Liverpool suburban stations enjoyed a very good timetable; Broad Green for instance had eleven trains to the city between 8.00am and 10.00am.

Stanier 4MT 2-6-4T No 42564 of Edge Hill shed, at Lime Street with empty stock for a main line working on the evening of 14th May 1956. Photograph J.A. Peden collection.

LIME STREET

For a century and a half Lime Street has been one of the most familiar station names in Britain and most travellers immediately associate it with Liverpool. Its origins go back to the early days of the Liverpool & Manchester company when Crown Street was proving inconvenient both in site and potential capacity. The Act for a branch from Edge Hill to Lime Street was obtained on 23rd May 1832. This sanctioned a tunnel nearly a mile long on a falling gradient of 1 in 93, the

LNWR 0-6-2T No 627 takes water at Lime Street, with the fireman in a rather precarious perch. These 'Coal Tanks' spent many years working passenger and empty stock trains into Lime Street and Riverside. No 627 was built in 1881 and lasted until 1927 without receiving its allotted LMS number. Photograph J.A. Sommerfield collection.

Stanier Pacific No 46203 PRINCESS MARGARET ROSE ready to leave Lime Street with the 2.00pm to Euston on Saturday 1st October 1960. The 'Princesses', far more than the 'Princess Coronations', were associated with Liverpool-London expresses from the 1930s to their withdrawal in 1961-62. The tender had been well filled for the 193 mile journey and the loco has a good head of steam for the 1 in 83/1 in 93 climb to Edge Hill. On occasions these fine engines worked 17 coach formations unaided. Note the smartly dressed 'spotters'! Happily, No 46203 is now preserved, Photograph E.V. Richards.

ST. GEORGE'S HALL

first proper train shed. The actual roof was of timber boarding with strips of windows at the apex and half way down each slope. This rested on large wooden trusses supported by longitudinal iron girders, in turn supported by arcades of cast iron columns along the platforms. Curved structural brackets between the upper parts of the columns created triangular spandrels which were treated decoratively, one of the most characteristic features of railway architecture in Victorian times.

Although this was the very first use of iron arcades in a station building, it had a precedent in metal framed churches such as St George at Everton. A simple Georgian block containing the booking office stood at the inner end of the tracks and amenity buildings on each platform gave the station symmetry. Liverpool Corporation's donation financed a handsome screen consisting of tall Roman arches and an impressive entrance flanked by Doric columns. Designed by John Foster, the city surveyor, it was com-

pleted in 1839 and eventually complemented St Georges Hall and the other classical buildings opposite.

Traffic increased substantially during the first ten years, so from 1846 to 1851 the terminus was extended and the tunnel mouth widened. William Tite designed blocks of Italianate buildings to replace the original Georgian structures and these were linked to Foster's screen by balustrades. As the number of passenger services multiplied, further expansion and a complete rebuilding became inevitable; this was carried out from 1867 to 1871 creating, more or less, the station as it is today. First to be tackled was the train shed. William Baker designed a pair of attractive elliptical roofs, 620 feet long, consisting of light girders springing from rather fat columns. They were wide (219

The far end of platform 7 at Lime Street was a favourite meeting place for local enthusiasts in the 1950s. On 31st March 1956 there were plenty of them about, ranging from schoolboys venturing into forbidden territory to senior members of the fraternity standing discreetly in the background. Their fascination with this rather dingy spot is more than apparent in this view. Royal Scot 4-6-0 No 46110 GRENADIER GUARDSMAN blasted out of Lime Street as it began to attack the climb towards Edge Hill with the 4.10pm for London Euston. Photograph Stanley Creer.

Recently ex-works, but only partially repainted, class 5 4-6-0 No 45412 makes a spirited departure from Lime Street with a parcels train, around 1952. Photograph J.A. Peden collection.

150 feet high chimney was built near Smithdown Lane towards the eastern end of the tunnel in an attempt to clear the smoke. This proved unsatisfactory, so the overlying rock was removed to create a spectacular cutting punctuated by no less than 25 bridges and short tunnels. This work was completed in 1881, and from 1885 to 1890 the excavation was widened to accommodate four tracks. The western portal had been modified earlier, with Copperas Hill and St Vincent Street carried across the station throat on massive stone and girder bridges.

At its maximum extent the station had eleven platforms numbered from the north, most of them between 650 feet and 700 feet long. With the 1867-71 rebuilding, all vestiges of symmetry disappeared and the waiting rooms, restaurant, refreshment rooms, telegraph office and other facilities either faced the concourse from the back of the hotel or extended along platform one. In July 1904 there were over five hundred scheduled arrivals and departures a day, plus North Wales holiday trains. Specials were arranged at short notice 'for a party of emigrants or American billionaires' according to a contemporary account. There was only a limited amount of suburban traffic at this time, but plenty of regular travellers to London - the annual season ticket to Euston cost £19.8s! Lime Street was always Liverpool's principal gateway to the rest of the country. In 1924 for example, besides the London expresses, there were departures for Glasgow, Edinburgh, Leeds, Newcastle, Hull, Holyhead, Aber-

feet and 166 feet respectively) but also gently curved, a combination which was particularly effective when viewed from the concourse. Despite its significance as an early example of civic planning, Foster's classical screen had to go. It was replaced by the huge North Western Hotel which opened on 1st March 1871 and incorporated station amenities on the platform side. Architect Alfred Waterhouse chose a distinctly vertical French Renaissance style, the 316 feet wide frontage being centred on towers capped by spires soaring 157 feet above the main entrance. Much of the architectural detail, includ-

ing whimsical statues of a king and queen, was too high to be noticed from the street however. The interior was particularly lavish, no doubt to satisfy discerning Americans. Besides some 300 bedrooms, there was an opulent entrance hall, a grand lounge, a sumptuous restaurant and a gentleman's smoking room.

Cable operation to Lime Street ceased in 1870, locomotives then hauling all trains out of the terminus. At first, one or more brake trucks were still placed at the head of incoming trains which thus descended by gravity. The use of steam traction brought ventilation problems and a

Lime Street on the evening of 26th May 1960. On the left Class 5 4-6-0 No 45429 is about to work the 5.20pm to Widnes Central. Stanier 2-6-4T No.42583 will haul the 5.32pm to Birkenhead Woodside, a circuitous journey via Runcorn, Helsby and Hooton ending up less than two miles away as the crow flies. 3F 0-6-0T No 47519 is the station pilot and 'Jubilee' 4-6-0 No 45558 MANITOBA is backing out to Edge Hill shed having arrived from Crewe. Photograph J.F. Ward.

ystwyth, Birmingham, Nottingham, Bristol, Swansea, Plymouth, Penzance and Brighton. An hourly service of 45 minute Manchester expresses was maintained and locals went to St Helens, Wigan, Widnes, Crewe, Chester, Garston, Alexandra Dock and Canada Dock. Over a million parcels passed through the station every year and a special bay was provided for unloading banana vans from Garston Dock. Perhaps the most remarkable traffic was that involving European emigrants bound for America around the turn of the century, a reminder that for the New World Liverpool was a Continental as well as an English port. Groups of Germans, Swedes, Poles and Russians passed through Lime Street carrying curious baggage and (in one porter's opinion) 'jabbering a lorra nice lingo'. The station master was responsible for 265 staff and a further hundred were employed in other departments.

Lime Street used to be a difficult station to work, despite the successive improvements. It was hemmed in by Lord

An impression of the Moorish Arch. Drawing by Juliet Whitworth.

Nelson Street to the north, Lime Street to the west, Skelhorne Street to the south, and the tunnel to the east, so further expansion and platform extensions were out of the question. Furthermore the concourse could hardly have been any narrower, so there was no scope for an extra few feet of track there either. In LMS days, long trains had to be made up in two sections, joined together immediately prior to departure. On arrival, tender locos were despatched to turntables near Sydney Street and Pellew Street close to the tunnel end of the platforms, whilst tank engines had to leave for Edge Hill as soon as possible or retire to limited siding accommodation adjacent to the turntables. A signal cabin just west of the tunnel mouth controlled some fifty signals, but inspectors on the ground supervised movements in and around the station. The end of cable operation resulted in more efficient working, but engines then had to blast up the incline to Edge Hill from a standing start. Departures from Lime Street were always noisy affairs and heavy trains were often banked out by the loco which had brought in the empty stock.

In 1836 the Liverpool & Manchester Railway opened a station at Edge Hill, on the Lime Street extension, to replace Wavertree Lane. It stood just east of the

The Edge Hill-Lime Street cutting, quadrupled in 1880-81, showing some of the massive bridges required for the numerous street crossings. Note the squinch arch on the nearest structure. The bare sandstone excavation is unfaced for most of its length; the same applied to Olive Mount cutting. The view was taken on 31st May 1975. Photograph D. Ibbotson.

tunnel mouth and was one of the earliest examples of purpose-built passenger facilities, other than a terminus. Driveways led down from Tunnel Road between curved stone walls and both platforms were furnished with identical buildings in local red sandstone. They were tall structures with prominent chimneys and large windows in the Tudor style. Around 1846-48 extensions were built, fortunately in complete harmony with the original design, and a light iron roof was erected over the tracks. Further additions were made in 1873. Most trains - including

some incoming expresses - stopped here, and 'To get off at Edge Hill' became a Liverpudlian euphemism for *coitus interruptus!* The station was cleaned up and restored to its former glory for the 1980 celebrations, but its unstaffed isolation rendered it vulnerable to mischief and the windows have had to be firmly boarded up. However, in 1996 Edge Hill celebrated 160 years of continuous use.

In summer 1995 there were 171 timetabled departures from Lime Street every weekday, including fourteen to London Euston, forming an hourly service for

Edge Hill station on 17th May 1980, looking towards Lime Street. One of the original Liverpool & Manchester Railway buildings is on the right. The sloping driveway leads to Tunnel Road. Photograph J.A. Sommerfield.

The north side of Edge Hill station on 9th July 1960, with 3F 0-6-0T No 47336 waiting to bank a train of vans up to the Gridiron reception sidings. The distant box is Waterloo Tunnel Mouth. To the left of it is the tunnel to Lime Street, whilst to the right of it smoke emerges from the long bore to Waterloo and Riverside. Photograph J.F. Ward.

Stanier 5MT 2-6-0 No 42984 of Nuneaton shed approaches the site of Speke station with a down freight on 23rd May 1959. The train is on the fast line and therefore destined for the Edge Hill complex. So called 'Table Bridge' in the background was a reminder of wartime defence measures, having once housed a gun emplacement. Photograph J.A. Peden collection.

most of the day. Other regular interval trains ran to Newcastle, Scarborough, Birmingham and Norwich, providing good links with most Yorkshire and Midland towns on the way. There were four or five services an hour to Manchester Piccadilly or Victoria and over thirty trains to Wigan. Through trains also ran to Blackpool, Barrow, Morecambe, Reading, Southampton, Bournemouth, Bristol, Cardiff and Plymouth, although notable through services losses are those to Scotland and North Wales. Platform shortening has allowed a larger concourse which is now very smart indeed and has direct access to the Merseytravel underground lines. A particularly pleasing feature is the view of the city through an etched glass screen. The North Western Hotel has been closed since 1933 and is a sad sight compared with smartened-up St Georges Hall opposite, but in 1996 re-furbishment as student accommodation commenced. A little bit of the past survives in the form of a short length of William Tite's balustrade next to Lord Nelson Street. One thing that has hardly changed at all for over a century is the contrast between the gloomy depths of the red sandstone approach cutting and the light airy spans of Lime Street's train shed, especially on a sunny day.

THE SOUTHERN APPROACH

Two and a half miles out of Lime Street and just over a mile from the tunnel, expresses to and from the south run along an embankment above the terraced streets of Wavertree. In the distance, above a sea of rooftops, the two cathedrals are a reminder that this is Liverpool and nowhere else. Over the years countless thousands of Liverpudlians must have looked out of carriage windows towards the Mersey - sad to leave, happy to be back, and doubtless vice versa in some instances. This impressive southern approach to the city was completed over a century and a quarter ago and has been taken for granted ever since, but its genesis was preceded by a lengthy saga of company rivalry involving numerous competing schemes and alliances made, broken and reinstated.

The idea of a railway from Merseyside to the south was first mooted in 1823, but Bills for a line from Birkenhead to Birmingham were thrown out of parliament in 1824 and 1826. Following the success of the Liverpool & Manchester Railway,

Class 5 4-6-0 No 45312 on the branch to Garston Dock, looking west on 21st August 1960. The train is carrying supports for the overhead wires leading to Garston Freightliner Terminal. The tall building on the left with its little used siding is Garston Gas Works. In the left foreground is the curving connection to Bryant & May's Mersey Match Works which closed in December 1994, the last such factory in Britain. Photograph J.F. Ward.

Garston Dock No 4 signal box, just north west of Dock Road, on 15th August 1971. The lines to the left lead to dockside sidings, identified by the cranes in the background. By this time many sidings in the middle distance had been lifted. Photograph J.A. Sommerfield.

pressure for a route to London became intense and the Grand Junction Railway obtained its Act on 6th May 1833. Trains from Lime Street to Birmingham Vauxhall via Earlestown, Warrington, Crewe, Stafford and Wednesfield Heath near Wolverhampton commenced on 4th July 1837 and connections to London Euston over the London & Birmingham Railway began on 24th June 1838. This comfort-

able monopoly of long distance Liverpool traffic was immediately threatened by the Chester & Crewe Railway and Birkenhead & Chester Railway which were sanctioned a few days either side of the Grand Junction opening. The established company retaliated by proposing a line from Moore (south of Warrington) to Huyton (on the Liverpool & Manchester) via a bridge across the Mersey at Fidler's Ferry. The

House of Commons was unimpressed and rejected this scheme, but to its considerable relief the Grand Junction managed to absorb the Chester & Crewe in July 1840, three months before the line opened.

These were volatile times and before long relations between the Grand Junction and Liverpool & Manchester became strained. The former nearly joined forces with the Great Western Railway, thus stirring up visions of broad gauge Paddington-Liverpool expresses. Instead it turned its attention to the Huyton short cut again. However, the Railway Mania of 1844-45 was throwing up all manner of schemes, including independent routes to Liverpool and Birkenhead. By mutual consent the Grand Junction absorbed the Liverpool & Manchester during 1845, in turn combining with the Manchester & Birmingham and London & Birmingham on 1st January 1846 to form the mighty London & North Western Railway, a force to be reckoned with. Just before its demise, the Grand Junction obtained powers for an even more direct short cut via a bridge at Runcorn Gap, but the LNWR balked at the cost and powers lapsed. Instead, by means of a series of clandestine treaties with other companies, rival lines from the south were kept out of Liverpool. This policy came to an end in 1858 with the resignation of Captain Huish, the LNWR's long standing chairman. The company then decided to consolidate its position in the city by more straightforward means and the scene was set for a direct ap-

Church Road station, Garston, looking south east towards the Speke-Garston Dock line on 5th October 1906. The station was open for passengers from 1881 to 1939, although the right hand buildings were demolished some time before closure. The line continued behind the camera to Garston Dock passenger station, where an end-on junction was made with a spur from the CLC main line. An LNWR 0-6-0ST with square tanks, converted from an 0-6-0 'Coal Engine', is shunting the line behind the station leading to Garston Dock goods. Photograph J. Ryan collection.

Caprotti class 5 4-6-0 No 44740 at Speke Junction on a Lime Street bound express, 27th August 1954. The lines branching to the right lead to Speke marshalling yard and the fine gantry spanning the quadruple main line can be seen in the distance. The photograph was taken from Speke Junction signal box. Photograph J.A. Peden collection.

proach at last. In 1860 attention turned to the railway through Warrington and Widnes on the north bank of the Mersey, a modest concern with early origins. Starting off as the St Helens & Runcorn Gap Railway in 1833, it amalgamated with the Sankey Brook Navigation in 1845 to form the St Helens Canal & Railway. With its dock at Runcorn Gap proving inadequate, the new company immediately sought powers for an extension to Garston further down the estuary. This annoyed the Grand Junction - which had thus far ig-

nored the local line - but in view of the proposed Runcorn bridge, the two companies agreed not to oppose each other's schemes. The Runcorn Gap-Garston line opened on 1st July 1852 and by 1854 tracks extended in the opposite direction to Warrington and Manchester. Between 1846 and 1856 this strategic route excited interest from the Midland, Great Western, Great Northern and North Staffordshire companies. Nevertheless, the LNWR leased the St Helens Canal & Railway on 14th June 1860 and sought powers for a

bridge at Fidler's Ferry again, but this plan was thrown out of parliament for a second time. So it was back to the expensive crossing at Runcorn Gap. An Act for the high level bridge there, together with a connection from Speke on the St Helens line to Edge Hill on the Liverpool & Manchester was acquired in 1861.

The line between Speke and Edge Hill, four and a half miles, was fairly easy to build and it opened on 15th February 1864, with intermediate stations at Allerton and Mossley Hill serving nearby villages. For three miles it was at or near ground level and only required shallow cuttings and a couple of road overbridges. The northern section ran on the embankment which now affords an extensive view of the city. On 29th July 1864 the St Helens company was absorbed by the LNWR. Construction of the massive Runcorn bridge, together with it long approach viaducts took six years, but it was eventually opened on 1st April 1869 and expresses ceased to grind round the sharp curve at Earlestown. Wavertree station opened on 1st September 1870 to serve the growing acres of terraced houses west of the embankment. The LNWR decided to develop the port of Garston and a direct curve from Allerton began to carry traffic on 1st January 1873. A new station called Garston Church Road, just short of the original St Helens terminus, opened on 1st March 1881 and the latter was simultaneously renamed Garston Dock. By this time the sheer number of passenger and goods trains on the main line was causing congestion, so quadru-

BR Standard 4MT 4-6-0 No 75013 passing Allerton station with a lengthy train, probably bound for North Wales, on 27th August 1954. Photograph J.A. Peden Collection.

The somewhat austere frontage of Mossley Hill station on Rose Lane, seen here in spring 1953. Posters advertise a Whit Monday excursion for ramblers to Mold, Rhydymwyn, Nannerch, Caerwys and Denbigh as well as a special train to London for the coronation of HM Queen Elizabeth II.

1939 and the local service from Lime Street to Garston Dock was withdrawn on 16th June 1947, having previously been suspended from 15th April 1917 to 5th May 1919. Rundown Wavertree conceded defeat to the buses on 5th August 1958 and Sefton Park followed on 2nd May 1960. Electrification using the 25,000 volts ac overhead system was completed on 18th June 1962, bringing new multiple units and light blue locomotives to the line. Mossley Hill, West Allerton and Allerton stations remain open and were served by 18 to 25 passenger trains each way on weekdays in summer 1995, formed of Sprinter and Pacer diesel units. Although the goods yard at Mossley Hill closed on 7th December 1964, freight is still handled at Garston Dock and for the time being quadruple track remains south of Edge Hill.

DOWN TO THE DOCKS

Although there was plenty of passenger traffic on the Liverpool & Manchester railway and even more when a main line to the south was established, the docks were the lifeblood of Merseyside and huge profits beckoned from the conveyance of imports and exports. Wapping depot was well placed for the old basins south of Pier Head, but most new developments were taking place in the opposite direction and by the mid-1840s newly promoted rival lines looked set to capture this business. Consequently, the first major LNWR project in Liverpool was an expensive branch, largely underground, from Edge Hill to the waterfront near Waterloo Dock. As the port expanded towards Bootle,

pling from Edge Hill to the Runcorn bridge approach viaduct became essential. This was completed in 1891 and Wavertree, Mossley Hill, Allerton and Speke stations were rebuilt with four platforms, plain booking offices and timber waiting rooms in typical LNWR fashion. Another station, to the same design, was opened at Sefton Park on 1st June 1892 to serve yet more terraces.

Between Wavertree and Allerton, southbound expresses were able to build up some speed after the climb out of Lime Street and the curve at Edge Hill, al-

though the junction at Speke had to be approached with caution. The succession of LNWR main line classes and LMS 4-6-0s and Pacifics were always an impressive sight in this part of Liverpool. Between the wars, suburban housing engulfed the fields of Allerton and to cater for the new residents, a starkly functional station opened at West Allerton, on 2nd January 1939. Retrenchment has been marked but not drastic. Speke station, still in splendid isolation at the time, was abandoned on 22nd September 1930. Garston Church Road closed on 3rd July

The spacious but fairly basic LNWR facilities at Mossley Hill in 1953, looking north from the main line island platform.

The entrance to Sefton Park station from the corner of Smithdown Road and Garmoyle Road, on 16th September 1958. A fine procession of cars, no doubt all painted black and considered vintage nowadays, headed towards the city centre. Cephos clearly cured more or less everything!

competing railways were in a better position to tap into the extra maritime traffic. So another bold scheme was embarked upon - this time a heavily engineered line from Edge Hill to Canada Dock, and eventually Alexandra Dock. Finally, the Waterloo branch acquired a new role when the Mersey Docks & Harbours Board opened its Riverside station for liner passengers. Initially this gave rise to the strange phenomenon whereby the most luxurious trains in the world threaded the gloomy interior of Waterloo goods depot. Waterloo, Victoria, Trafalgar and Clarence Docks opened between 1830 and 1836, the first manifestation of the expansion northwards, and they were well established by the time the LNWR was formed. With a

line along the dock road from Wapping completely unacceptable at the time, the only way of reaching them was by means of a tunnel diagonally under the city from Edge Hill. There were actually two tunnels, Victoria (1 mile 947 yards) beginning immediately alongside Edge Hill station, and Waterloo (850 yards) leading to the goods depot on Waterloo Road. Between them was a 70 yard 'lung' bordered by Byron Street and Fontenoy Street in the St Anne's district. Construction was further complicated by the need to take the line down accurately at 1 in 56 and 1 in 60 to emerge level with the quays. New stationary engines were built at Edge Hill and these also took over operation of the Lime Street and Wapping inclines. At Byron

Street short spurs equipped with sand drags were installed in case of runaways on the two and a half mile double track branch. Traffic began on 1st August 1849, a connection to the dock estate opening in 1858. After successive enlargements, Waterloo goods became a huge gloomy depot, extending for 640 feet from Great Howard Street to Waterloo Road and having a breadth of no less than 550 feet between Oil Street and Formby Street.

Within three years of the Waterloo branch becoming operational the port had expanded northwards for well over a mile, Huskisson Dock being completed in 1852. Much to the chagrin of the LNWR this was deep in L & Y territory and further developments could only strengthen the position of the opposition. When Canada Dock opened in 1860, Euston decided that it was essential to invest some capital in a line to the north Mersey quays. The result was a heavily engineered and very expensive piece of railway, but one which has largely survived intact for a hundred and thirty years.

The five mile Bootle branch commenced a thousand yards east of Edge Hill station and immediately curved sharply left. A dead straight northerly alignment for exactly two miles took the tracks firstly through a shallow cutting spanned by Edge Lane and Prescot Road, then on a low embankment punctuated by bridges across West Derby Road and Townsend Lane. (The latter was once the main road to Manchester.) Next came a sweeping ninety degree curve to the west between Anfield and Walton. At City Road the branch was only a mile and a half from the docks, but most of the money had yet to be spent because of the intervening sandstone ridge. Excavations began with a sheer walled rock cutting bridged by County Road, followed by Spellow Tunnel at 347 yards. A gaping cutting, eventually overlooked by the back yards of Selwyn Street and Cairo Street, led to Westminster Road No.1 Tunnel (62 yards) and Westminster No.2 (276 yards). When the CLC Huskisson branch was built a few years later, it spanned the intervening gap by means of a plate girder bridge. Kirkdale station on the L & Y was directly above Westminster Road No.2 Tunnel. Another short but deep cutting, this time between the terraces of Argos Road and the L & Y Bank Hall loco shed, led to Canada Dock Tunnel (427 yards) which passed beneath Bank Hall station and the Leeds & Liverpool Canal. Immediately beyond the waterway, the tracks emerged in an extensive goods yard spanned by viaducts carrying Bankhall Lane and Derby Road. Thankfully Canada Dock was now just a few hundred yards away.

Services began in a modest way on 1st June 1866 with goods workings as far as Stanley and passenger trains from Lime Street to Stanley and Tue Brook. The line opened for goods traffic throughout on

A Lime Street-bound express rushes through Wavertree station on 14th October 1958. The original Edge Hill-Speke line is on the left and later tracks to the right, bridges over Wellington Road clearly showing the different construction phases.

Ex-LNWR 0-8-0 No 49130 of Edge Hill shed, complete with tender cab, returns to the depot along the Bootle branch near Stanley on 26th June 1962. The hopper wagons will be empties from Lister Drive Power Station. Photograph E.V. Richards.

15th October 1866 but passenger services to Bootle (Canada Dock) together with intermediate stations at Breck Road and Walton for Aintree had to wait until 1st July 1870. Edge Lane was added in November 1870, for passenger traffic only.

Station buildings reflected current LNWR architectural practice, but they were a varied lot. Stanley and Tue Brook had standard wooden structures featuring horizontal planking, hipped roofs and heavy canopies. Walton for Aintree, possibly in deference to medieval Walton on the Hill and probably because of aspirations to serve the distant racecourse, received special treatment. Although still basically timber shells, the buildings boasted steeper roofs, decorative ridge tiles, enormous finials and distinctive chimneys. One of them even had a neat dormer gable over the clock. At Edge Lane the platform accommodation was brick built and displayed very tall chimneys, chamfered ends to the roofs and alternate red and cream bricks above the round arched windows - pleasant touches for a humdrum suburban station. Canada Dock was frankly disappointing. It had a solitary platform stretching between Bankhall Lane and Derby Road and a single storey red brick building fronting the latter. This was carried on a girder deck supported by iron columns and had a modicum of cream brickwork around the windows. Access to the platform was by means of a stairway at the back of the booking office.

For once the LNWR anticipated new port developments and gained access to Atlantic Dock in Bootle before the quays were complete. Goods traffic began to use the line on 1st January 1880 and the basin opened as Alexandra Dock, after a last minute change of name, in September 1881. The new railway began at Atlantic Dock Junction, deep in the cutting between Westminster Road No.2 and Canada Dock tunnels, and was another expensive project. The junction signal box retained its original name until closure over a century later. From Atlantic Dock Junction the branch, a mile and a quarter long, curved northwards through Oriel Road Tunnel (288 yards) which passed beneath romantically named Falstaff Street, Portia Street and Romeo Street. It emerged alongside the L & Y Southport line and ran parallel to it as far as Balliol Road. A curve to the west then took the line through Berry Street Tunnel (140 yards) almost below Oriel Road station. A short gap of 33 yards, involving the demolition of some terraced houses in Berry Street and Canal Street led to Alexandra Dock Tunnel (117 yards). The line emerged just beyond the Leeds & Liverpool Canal, then curved northwards under Derby Road to an extensive goods yard parallel to Regent Road.

Passenger services from Lime Street to Alexandra Dock (actually Atlantic Dock for five days) commenced on 5th September 1881, the intermediate station at Balliol Road opening on the same date. Like Canada Dock, the terminus at Alexandra Dock had just one platform, although it also boasted a generous overall roof supported on iron columns and lattice girders. A single storey building in red brick with the usual mild decoration faced Regent Road. Balliol Road station, although handy for the centre of Bootle, was severely constrained by its site in a cutting. Furthermore, the platforms lay on a curve and were pinched in the middle by a big sandstone arch carrying the road known as Millers Bridge. A booking office in the now-familiar LNWR style faced Bootle Town Hall, which was still being built at the time, and paths led down to little waiting rooms, one either side of the bridge.

Spellow station, opened in September 1882 on the original Canada Dock line, presented an even greater challenge to the designers. The line was in a deep sandstone cutting with vertical walls at this point, and access to the platforms demanded some ingenuity. The booking office on County Road, with its chamfered gables and prominent chimneys, was reminiscent of the style adopted for Edge Lane. From the rear of it a stairway descended to a footbridge across the tracks which in turn led to steps down to either platform, all of these passageways being enclosed by timber and glass. Such drastic measures were prompted by the spread of terraced housing, some fifty streets in all, within half a mile of the station site.

Back at Edge Hill, a spur between Olive Mount Junction and Edge Lane Junction, involving the 147 yard Olive Mount Tunnel, opened on 11th July 1883, enabling goods trains from the Earlestown and Manchester direction to reach Bootle. A straightforward connection between the adjacent LNWR and L & Y tracks south of Balliol Road was brought into operation on 1st May 1886, allowing through

Tue Brook station in July 1939 with an ex-LNWR 'Watford Tank', LMS No 6866, on an Alexandra Dock to Lime Street train. The engine was built in 1898 and withdrawn in May 1946, two years before local passenger traffic ceased on the Bootle branch. Bovril is still available today, but Virol and Palethorpes Sausages seem to have vanished! Photograph J. Gahan.

coaches to be run from Euston to Southport.

Although there was a fair amount of residential traffic to Lime Street from the suburban stations between Spellow and Edge Lane, the Alexandra and Canada Dock branches were very much bound up with the waterfront. Most trains carried dockers and those employed in quayside industries to and from work, and some services ran in the early hours of the morning. Goods traffic reached enormous levels and the facilities to accommodate it were in proportion. Huge multi-storey warehouses consisting of an iron column and girder framework clad with decora- tive brickwork reared above the puny pas- senger stations at Canada Dock and Alexandra Dock. Connections to the quays all the way from Huskisson to Hornby via the dock line ensured a regular flow of traffic to these mammoth depots.

Lime Street was well placed for the com- mercial heart of the city but was decid- edly inconvenient for the thousands of trans-Atlantic voyagers passing through Liverpool each month. With the Waterloo branch perfectly suited to passenger trains to the docks, providing a few modi- fications were carried out, the LNWR and MD & HB decided to revolutionise the arrangement for dealing with liner traf- fic. Locomotives replaced cable working through the tunnel from 16th February 1895 and the Harbour Board's Riverside station on the seaward side of Prince's Dock opened on 12th June 1895. Although this had all the architectural merits of a transit shed, it fulfilled its role perfectly. There were two main platforms, 795 feet and 698 feet respectively, with a centre track and crossovers at the inner ends for engine release purposes. Also sheltered by the full length overall roof and brick side walls was a 560 feet bay on the eastern side. There were waiting rooms beyond the buffers, but other facilities normally associated with an important terminus were absent - refreshments were avail- able on the boat trains and with no local customers a booking office, left luggage room and the like were unnecessary. Trains approached the station through Waterloo depot, along the MD & HB line in Waterloo Road and over a swing bridge across the entrance to Prince's Dock.

Only LNWR boat trains used Riverside station and prior to World War 1 these included the prestigious 'American Spe- cials' from Euston. At the turn of the cen- tury there were two trains a week con- necting with White Star and Cunard sailings. They ran non-stop to Edge Hill in 3 hours 45 minutes and were allowed a further 15 minutes to reach Riverside, punctuality being an absolute priority. Hotels in London were canvassed so that the numbers of passengers could be esti- mated, then a third more accommodation than was deemed necessary provided, to avoid overcrowding. In summer there could be up to two hundred first class passengers as well as fifty or so in second and third class.

The very attractive station buildings at Walton, looking south in the early 1900s. Its 'for Aintree' appendix was rather optimistic, this district being well over two miles away. Presumably complaints from passengers led to the renaming as Walton & Anfield in 1910. Pears Soap and Epps' Cocoa advertisements are evident. Photograph J. Ryan collection.

The train included first class corridor coaches, saloons with drawing rooms and smoking rooms, dining and kitchen cars, and luggage vans. Two meal sittings were provided for first class and luncheon baskets were available for other passengers. The clientele included the rich and famous as well as characters as diverse as a New York judge musing over the small size of English trains to hardened poker players occupying a saloon well before the train started.

In 1948 there were still up to four specials a day. Because these had to negotiate busy Waterloo Road and the swingbridge across Prince's Dock (which was frequently opened for coastal shipping) special arrangements were necessary. A typical operation for departing trains was as follows. Firstly, BR staff were informed of the expected docking time of a ship and the number of passengers booked through to London. The train departure time was decided, a path arranged to Euston and Edge Hill instructed to organise rolling stock. The special sets maintained by the LNWR had long gone, and ordinary main line coaches were used, although meals in the restaurant car were reputedly better than on ordinary services! Eventually the empty train arrived, followed by the ship, and boarding was completed. Express locos were not allowed on to the dock lines until track realignment and strengthening of the swingbridge was carried out between October 1949 and March 1950. For over fifty years the boat trains were entrusted to a pair of Webb tank engines as far as Edge Hill and the leading one proudly sported main line passenger headlamps for the short journey.

Departure from Riverside was at walking pace and drivers had a difficult task starting 300 ton trains on the sharp curve out of the station and across Prince's Dock swingbridge. This had a two way signal with arms at right angles - one for the railway and the other for shipping. As the train eased into Waterloo Road a pilotman holding a red flag preceded it - a scene reminiscent of the very early days of railways and almost bizarre for an express which would soon to be travelling at 70mph. Meanwhile, a policeman held up traffic on the dock road. After starting to build up speed through the blatantly commercial surroundings of Waterloo depot (this must have been a strange introduction to Britain for first time visitors) the two tanks attacked the incline up to Edge Hill. Foul air inside the tunnel often caused discomfort on the footplate and occasionally the engines stalled, so a third 0-6-2T had to be summoned from Edge Hill to rescue the train. Ex-LMS class 5 4-6-0s and 'Super D' 0-8-0s of LNWR vintage eased matters after 1950, but traffic soon began to wane.

The LNWR dock branches performed a vital role during the two world wars. Riverside station saw hundreds of thousands of troop movements whilst enormous qualities of munitions and supplies passed through Alexandra and Canada Depots. However, the 1940-41 blitz caused havoc at the north Mersey termini. In the most severe air raid on Liverpool thus far, Alexandra Dock warehouse was totally destroyed during the early hours of 20th December 1940, although the passenger service managed to carry on. Canada Dock station expired in a spectacular way before daybreak on 4th May 1941. The goods warehouse was gutted in a massive fire and high explosives breached the Leeds & Liverpool Canal embankment, flooding the railway yards and forcing a shunting engine to make a hasty retreat into the tunnel. Debris covering the sidings was quickly removed, but the already pared down passenger service was never reinstated. Waterloo also suffered badly and had to be patched up, the same applying to Riverside.

Passenger services from Alexandra Dock to Lime Street were temporarily withdrawn on 31st May 1948 and the shutdown became permanent on 26th February 1949. This involved the closure of intermediate stations at Bootle Balliol Road (the full name was adopted in January 1891), Spellow, Walton & Anfield (renamed in January 1910), Breck Road, The Brook, Stanley and Edge Lane. Local goods facilities continued, but were eventually abandoned piecemeal: Walton on 7th December 1964, Tue Brook on 27th November 1967 and Breck Road on 8th September 1969, for example. The large depots, or what remained of them, fell

WD 2-8-0 No 90527 of Aintree shed raises the echoes through the decrepit remains of Spellow station on 16th June 1958, ten years after passenger facilities were withdrawn. The main building was on County Road, the principal route to Preston and the north. Photograph J.A. Peden collection.

Remarkable structural work on the Bootle branch between Spellow and Atlantic Dock Junction, looking east on 31st May 1975. The LNWR tracks are at the lowest level. Note the unusual vaulting supporting the junction of Westminster Road and Melrose Road. The photograph was taken from a plate girder bridge carrying CLC tracks to Huskisson goods yard. Immediately off to the left, at a higher level again, is Kirkdale station on the L & Y main line out of Exchange. Photograph D. Ibbotson.

victim to the decline in freight traffic from the docks. Waterloo closed on 30th September 1963, except for a siding serving adjacent seed mills which lasted for a couple more years. The gaunt derelict shell remained in the late 1980s, but the site was finally redeveloped in 1995. Alexandra Dock finished on 2nd January 1967 and the area was still wasteland nearly thirty years later. Canada Dock lasted until 3rd September 1982 and the long closed passenger station survived for another ten years until new building work began. This particular closure meant the end of Atlantic Dock Junction, where the lonely signal box had been destroyed by a malicious fire in July 1980, having suffered similar attacks in 1950 and 1976.

Riverside station, which had latterly seen only about two trains a month, closed officially on 1st March 1971. The last working, a Northern Ireland troop special, was actually on 25th February. Grand National specials continued to use the Bootle branch as far as Bootle Junction, with a diesel taking over at Edge Hill where the train reversed. Lime Street-Southport railcars also followed the same route until 9th October 1977 when Merseyrail electrics began to serve Lime Street underground station. Fortunately the Bootle branch was saved by the construction of a siding into Seaforth Container Depot, an idea which had first been mooted in the late 1960s. From 12th February 1980 Freightliners regularly eased across Regent Road and past the site of Alexandra Dock station en route for the Garston terminal where the boxes were

transferred to other services. There is now a daily train through the Channel Tunnel from Garston. The Bootle branch also carries an increasing amount of imported coal via the recently constructed Seaforth Coal Terminal. Finally, the spur from Olive Mount Junction was closed on 28th February 1987, when Edge Lane Junction signal box was burnt down.

EDGE HILL

From 1850 to 1890 the area east of Edge Hill station became one of the most complex railway sites in the world, and remained a hive of activity for another seventy years. It was all very different in 1820 when the area was described as 'a health resort with fresh air and bracing breezes' and Wavertree Road was 'a beautiful avenue lined with tall trees'. Edge Lane was one of the original packhorse roads out of Liverpool and provided a rural route through farmland. A few houses grew up near Crown Street after the Liverpool & Manchester Railway opened, but for several decades the only dwellings east of here were Spekefield cottages, built near Edge Hill station in the 1840s for railwaymen. Thirty years on, the city was beginning to spread across the fields of Edge Hill and Wavertree with a vengeance. The wedge between Smithdown Road and Tunnel Road was built up during the 1870s, the area between Edge Lane and Wavertree Road followed in the 1880s, and the massive development south east of Edge Hill station was completed by the late 1890s. Over two hundred streets, with many thousands of

houses, had appeared in just thirty years.

From the early days of the Liverpool & Manchester Railway there were sidings at Edge Hill to deal with wagons brought up from Wapping, and the demand for accommodation increased relentlessly, especially after the Waterloo branch opened. In 1850 goods traffic despatched from Edge Hill amounted to 257,025 tons and the yards occupied forty acres with space for 1,782 wagons. The Bootle branch generated even more business and during 1873 1,032,853 tons of merchandise left the sidings, which by now covered 104 acres and held 3,215 wagons. However, this meant that a four-fold increase in traffic had to be handled by less than double the capacity, leading to great difficulties. The exchange of wagons between various groups of sidings often involved crossing the main lines, and this was downright hazardous at busy periods or in poor weather. With the safety of passenger trains paramount, the LNWR had to bear the burden of serious delays to goods traffic. Furthermore, as the sidings multiplied, forming trains became more complex. Sets of wagons arrived from different directions and each set usually had several trucks for various groups of tracks.

The solution was bold, intriguing and expensive. It incorporated two distinct but totally interdependent elements - firstly the double-track circular high level goods line and its associated spurs; secondly an extensive marshalling yard incorporating the famous 'gridiron'. Construction of the massive layout began in 1873 and took over two decades to complete, although much of it was in place within eight years.

The circular tracks, completed in 1882, began just north of Wavertree station on the route from Runcorn and Speke. They rose steadily on the west side of the main line before curving eastwards on an embankment, the passenger tracks being spanned by a girder bridge. After heading almost due east for a short distance, the goods lines described a sweeping 180 degree curve, crossing the Manchester route and the Bootle branch on the way. By now they were heading west and descending towards Picton Road Junction where they joined the Waterloo line. Two important spurs were built as well. A link from Engine Shed Junction (originally Lodging House Junction) snaked across the entrance to Edge Hill engine shed on a viaduct and met the Wapping branch at Edge Hill No 4 signal box. This line facilitated transfers between yards on the northern and southern sides of the complex, but in theory could be used by a most unlikely through service between Waterloo and Wapping! The other link was from remote Exhibition Junction (on the ascent from Picton Road) to Pighue Lane Junction (on the Bootle branch Edge Lane - Olive Mount spur) and provided easy access to the Manchester line. Incidentally, Exhibition Junction was named after the International Exhibition of Navigation, Travel, Commerce and Manufacture, held in the grounds of nearby Edge Lane Hall during 1886. It was opened by Queen Victoria, attracted three million visitors and included parades of llamas, a model of the Eddystone lighthouse and an Indian village with forty natives specially imported for the occasion!

The marshalling yards were laid out on 70 acres of spare LNWR land to the north of the Manchester line. As the ground sloped gradually from east to west, gravity for sorting the wagons offered itself as an option. Although this method was in use at places such as Jarrow and Shildon in the North East, it had never been employed on such a scale, nor had a site been specially adapted. Over two million cubic yards of subsoil and rock had to be redistributed. Picko No.1 Tunnel (52 yards) and Picko No.2 (167 yards) were created so that the Bootle branch could pass beneath the site, and £2 million of LNWR cash was spent on the project. The complex was a mile in length and contained nearly sixty miles of track.

At the eastern or upper end near Olive Mount there were six reception sidings holding 294 wagons where trip workings arrived from Wapping, Waterloo and Bootle. Next came 24 sorting sidings in two groups, into which trucks for particular districts were despatched, irrespective of order. These could hold 1,065 wagons. Then came the marshalling sidings, comprising the pairs of gridirons where trains were arranged in station order. Finally, within sight of Edge Hill station, were four departure lines with a capacity of 188 wagons or four trains.

When a trip arrived at the reception lines the brakes were secured, a sorting siding number chalked on each wagon and the engine detached. A yardman then uncoupled and released the trucks, calling out the chalked number to a colleague who passed on the information by hand signals to the shunter in charge of the points. At night, red, white and green glasses on hand lamps conveyed information between shunters.

Gradients ranged from 1 in 100 on straight track to 1 in 50 on curves at the lower end of each gridiron, and varied according to the acceleration required of a wagon or the resistance met by it. In theory the speed of a truck could be accurately predicted by shunters and adjusted if necessary. However, no two vehicles ran exactly the same. Some companies kept their stock in better order than others so the condition of tyres and axle boxes varied considerably. Loads of round timber and iron beams on two or more flat wagons caused very stiff running round the curves. Lime trucks often suffered from clogged axle boxes, strong westerly wind slowed covered vans and short wheelbase wagons with heavy loads ran very freely in hot weather.

Speed could be very effectively controlled by brake poles thrust between the wheel spring and brake lever, but there were sometimes runaways. On such occasions the remarkable 'chain drag' was brought into operation. This consisted of a steel hook attached to a heavy cable running in a ballast-filled trough between the rails. When the hook engaged an axle, the drag of the cable arrested speeding trucks in a matter of seconds. It was used 206 times from June 1875 to June 1895 and halted runaways every time, without damage to the wagons or their contents.

Evocatively named Atlantic Dock Junction signal box, looking west towards Stanley Road. The 1866 line to Canada Dock is on the left, whilst the 1880 route to Alexandra Dock curves away to the right. The latter remains open for traffic to Seaforth Coal and Freightliner Terminals. In this view, 17th August 1971, the derelict land on the left marks the rear of former Bank Hall loco shed. Photograph J.A. Sommerfield.

Atlantic Dock Junction signal box, looking east in the 1930s. In the distance is Westminster Road No.2 Tunnel which passes beneath the former L & Y Kirkdale station. A train is signalled for Alexandra Dock and this will pass to the left of the box. Photograph D. Ibbotson.

The remains of Bootle Balliol Road station on the Alexandra Dock line, photographed on 20th August 1971. Cramped side platforms were in the cutting, whilst the former booking office can still be seen on the right. Bootle Oriel Road station on the L & Y Liverpool-Southport line is just to the north. Photograph J.A. Sommerfield.

In 1894 the Edge Hill gridiron dealt with 1,226,303 tons of traffic and by 1904 this had reached 1,275,009 tons. The record number of wagons to pass through in a 24 hour period was 2,928, although the average was 2,200. Every day about 150 wagons passing through the gridiron did not leave as part of a train; these included 'cripples' destined for the repair shops and trucks carrying material for LNWR internal use. The yard employed 81 men and work followed a daily cycle, increasing from 11.00am, peaking at 10.30pm, and tailing off after 6.30am when the last train left. The whole layout was equipped with a comprehensive system of electric lighting in 1909. Interest in the gridiron was worldwide and there were numerous visits by foreign railway representatives. From the 1870s to the early 1900s several other railway facilities grew up in spaces between the running lines and sidings or were tucked away in corners of the vast Edge Hill complex. Particularly important was the huge engine shed which eventually had no less than twenty roads under cover and was approached, most unusually, through six arches in one of the goods line viaducts. Just to the south, a large coaling plant and two turntables occupied the angle between the circular route near Engine Shed Junction and the main line south. Further west, beyond six streets of terraced houses, was the fruit and vegetable depot facing Tunnel Road. Spekeland Road depot, dealing with hay for Liverpool's numerous working horses and coal for its domestic hearths, was further down Tunnel Road. Cattle destined for the city's abattoirs were dealt with at pens near Picton Road, whilst nearby private sidings led to an ironworks, bottle factory and Wavertree gasworks. A wagon repair shop stood just west of the gridiron and a seven road carriage cleaning shed was squeezed between the Wapping branch and Edge Hill station.

The decline of the gridiron and Edge Hill generally reflected the eclipse of Liverpool as a port - although the increasing role of road transport had been a factor since the 1930s. Retrenchment really set in during the 1960s and 1970s, but when the once incredibly busy Picton Road Junction signal box at the western end of the erstwhile gridiron closed in May 1982 it was abundantly clear that the famous LNWR enterprise had gone for good. The line from Engine Shed Junction to Picton Road had closed in October 1981 and the remaining part of the circular goods route - from Wavertree to Engine Shed Junction - finished in June 1983. Edge Hill shed, by then just a fuelling and inspection point for diesel locos, was closed at the same time.

Today the abandoned tunnel mouths, rock cuttings, arches and red sandstone viaducts briefly seen from an incoming express are reminiscent of some vast archaeological site. They also provide an irresistible adventure playground for local youngsters and several boys have been electrocuted while playing on the roofs of derelict coaches. Wavertree Technology Park now occupies parts of the gridiron, an appropriate use in view of the pioneering nature of the marshalling yard in the 1870s.

DEPARTURES FROM LIVERPOOL LIME STREET

Monday to Saturday, July 1960
SO - Saturdays Only
SX - Saturdays Excepted
FO - Fridays Only
Liverpool Riverside departures were not shown in the timetable, but services from Lime Street such as THE SHAMROCK and THE MANXMAN which connected with Dublin, Belfast and Isle of Man steamers had their own listings.
12.05 am London Euston (Sleeping cars, Mondays excepted)
12.45 am Glasgow Central (Sleeping cars)
5.50am Leeds City
5.58am Runcorn
6.10am Wigan North Western
6.34am Rock Ferry (via Helsby)
6.40am Wigan North Western
7.15am Chester General (Llandudno SO)
7.20am Kenyon Junction
7.26am Wigan North Western
7.30am SX Stafford
7.40am Wigan North Western
7.42am SO Llandudno
7.45am Manchester Exchange

Alexandra Dock passenger station seen from Regent Road on 22nd August 1955. A modest booking office in the contemporary LNWR style was provided, but the large overall roof was exceptional for a dock branch terminus. Its ample dimensions were misleading, for the roof merely sheltered a single platform. Note the fine mechanical horse and trailer.

7.50am SX Bangor
7.50am SO Birmingham New Street
7.58am SX Warrington Bank Quay
8.03am SO Warrington Bank Quay
8.05am SX London Euston THE SHAM-ROCK (Restaurant Car)
8.10am SX Birmingham New Street
8.15am SO London Euston THE SHAM-ROCK (Restaurant Car)
8.25am SX Wigan North Western
8.25am SO St Helens Shaw Street
8.25am SX Pwllheli
8.25am SO Runcorn
8.35am SO Paignton/Penzance
9.00am Newcastle (Restaurant Car)
9.05am Plymouth/Torquay/Paignton/Kingswear (Restaurant Car)

9.10am Wigan North Western
9.15am SO Llandudno
9.30am SO Penychain (for Butlins Camp)
9.40am St Helens Shaw Street
9.50am SO London Euston
10.00am London Euston THE MERSEY-SIDE EXPRESS (Restaurant Car, through coaches from Southport Chapel Street)
10.05am SX Bournemouth West (Restaurant Car from Crewe)
10.05am SO Birmingham New Street
10.10am Wigan North Western
10.20am SO Bournemouth West
10.30am SO Llandudno
10.35am Chester General

10.40am St Helens Shaw Street
11.00am London Euston (Restaurant Car, through coaches from Southport Chapel Street SO)
11.10am Wigan North Western
11.35am SO Rugby Midland (attached to London Euston train at Crewe)
11.40am St Helens Shaw Street
11.45am SX Birmingham New Street/Rugby Midland (attached to London Euston train at Crewe)
12.05pm SX Warrington Bank Quay
12.05pm SO Manchester Oxford Road
12.10pm Wigan North Western
12.15pm SO Warrington Bank Quay
12.40pm St Helens Shaw Street
12.40pm SO Llandudno
1.00pm Manchester Exchange
1.05pm SO London Euston
1.10pm Wigan North Western
1.30pm SO Bangor
1.35pm SX Chester General
1.40pm St Helens Shaw Street
1.45pm SO London Euston
1.55pm SO London Euston THE MANXMAN (Buffet Car)
2.00pm SX London Euston THE MANXMAN (Buffet Car)
2.05pm SO Newcastle
2.10pm Wigan North Western
2.20pm Newcastle (Buffet Car)
2.40pm St Helens Shaw Street
2.50pm Birmingham New Street/Cardiff General
3.10pm Wigan North Western
3.28pm SX Chester General
3.30pm SO Chester General
3.40pm St Helens Shaw Street
3.50pm Hull (Buffet Car)
4.00pm London Euston (through coaches from Southport Chapel Street)
4.10pm Wigan North Western

Sixteen years after closure, Alexandra Dock station still survived in ramshackle condition in June 1964. Even the nameboard was in place. The site was subsequently cleared and is now open ground. However, a single track serving the flourishing Seaforth Coal and Freightliner Terminal still passes to the right of this view. Photograph C.H.A. Townley.

The austere frontage of Riverside station in Saint Nicholas Place, 17th August 1971. Although owned by the Mersey Docks & Harbour Board, it was exclusively used by LNWR/LMS/BR boat trains from 1895 until 1971. A poster to the right of the entrance advertises an excursion to the Isle of Man for £2-20! The buildings have now been completely demolished. Photograph J.A. Sommerfield.

4.10pm SX Crewe
4.10pm SO Birmingham New Street
4.25pm SX Llandudno/Afon Wen
4.25pm SO Llandudno
4.40pm SX Wigan North Western
4.40pm SO St Helens Shaw Street
4.43pm SX Manchester Oxford Road
4.50pm Earlestown
4.50pm SX Birmingham New Street
5.00pm Holyhead
5.00pm Newcastle (Restaurant Car)
5.15pm London Euston THE RED
ROSE (Restaurant Car)
5.15pm Wigan North Western
5.20pm SX Warrington Bank Quay
5.22pm SO Wigan North Western
5.25pm SX Wigan North Western
5.32pm SX Birkenhead Woodside (via
Helsby)
5.35pm Earlestown
5.40pm SO St Helens Shaw Street
5.45pm London Euston (Restaurant Car
Crewe to London SO)
5.50pm SX St Helens Shaw Street
6.00pm SX Warrington Bank Quay
6.10pm Wigan North Western
6.15pm Manchester Exchange
6.20pm Chester General
6.30pm SO Warrington Bank Quay
6.40pm SO St Helens Shaw Street
6.53pm Warrington Bank Quay
7.00pm Birmingham New Street/Bristol
Temple Meads
7.00pm Leeds City
7.10pm Wigan North Western
7.20pm Crewe
7.40pm Chester General
7.40pm SO St Helens Shaw Street
8.10pm Wigan North Western
8.35pm Leeds City
8.40pm SO St Helens Shaw Street

8.45pm SO Birmingham New Street
(via Stoke on Trent)
9.10pm Wigan North Western
9.10pm SX Chester General
9.25pm SO Chester General
10.10pm Crewe
10.10pm St Helens Shaw Street
10.30pm Chester General
10.35pm Leeds City/York
10.35pm Wigan North Western
10.45pm Newton-le-Willows
11.10pm St Helens Shaw Street
11.30pm FO Penzance
11.45pm Cardiff General

**EDGE HILL (8A) SHED ALLOCA-
TION JANUARY 1954**
Ex-LMS Fairburn 4MT 2-6-4T: 42121
Ex-LMS Stanier 4MT 2-6-4T: 42426,
42459, 42564, 42570, 42583, 42596,
42602
Ex-LMS Stanier 5MT 4-6-0: 44768,
44769, 44772, 44773, 44906, 44907,
45020, 45039, 45069, 45111, 45113,
45181, 45242, 45243, 45249, 45250,
45256, 45276, 45303, 45305, 45343,
45373, 45376, 45380, 45388, 45393,
45398, 45399, 45413, 45421
**Ex-LMS Fowler 6P/Ivatt 7P Rebuilt
(*) 'Patriot' 4-6-0:** 45515 CAERNAR-
VON, 45518 BRADSHAW, 45521 *
RHYL, 45525 * COLWYN BAY, 45527 *
SOUTHPORT, 45531 * SIR
FREDERICK HARRISON, 45533 LORD
RATHMORE, 45534 * E TOOTAL
BROADHURST, 45538 GIGGLESWICK,
45550
Ex-LMS Stanier 6P 'Jubilee' 4-6-0:
45567 SOUTH AUSTRALIA, 45596
BAHAMAS, 45606 FALKLAND IS-

LANDS, 45613 KENYA, 45623 PALES-
TINE, 45670 HOWARD OF
EFFINGHAM, 45681 ABOUKIR, 45721
IMPREGNABLE
**Ex-LMS Stanier 7P 'Royal Scot'
4-6-0:** 46123 ROYAL IRISH FUSILIER,
46124 LONDON SCOTTISH, 46135
THE EAST LANCASHIRE REGIMENT,
46149 THE MIDDLESEX REGIMENT,
46152 THE KING'S DRAGOON
GUARDSMAN, 46153 THE ROYAL
DRAGOON, 46158 THE LOYAL REGI-
MENT, 46164 THE ARTISTS' RIFLE-
MAN
**Ex-LMS Stanier 8P 'Princess Royal'
4-6-2:** 46200 THE PRINCESS ROYAL,
46204 PRINCESS LOUISE, 46205
PRINCESS VICTORIA, 46207 PRIN-
CESS ARTHUR OF CONNAUGHT,
46208 PRINCESS HELENA VICTORIA
Ex-LMS 3F 0-6-0T: 47325, 47353,
47357, 47385, 47392, 47402, 47404,
47407, 47411, 47416, 47487, 47489,
47498, 47519, 47597
Ex-LMS Stanier 8F 2-8-0: 48260,
48457, 48512, 48513
Ex-LNWR/LMS 7F 0-8-0: 48932,
49082, 49137, 49173, 49200, 49224,
49314, 49355, 49368, 49375, 49392,
49394, 49399, 49404, 49412, 49419,
49423, 49427, 49429, 49434, 49437,
49445
Ex-L&Y Aspinall 2F 0-6-0ST: 51313,
51353, 51445
Ex-L&Y Aspinall 3F 0-6-0: 52140,
52321

Total allocation 115

Riverside Railway Station. LIVERPOOL.

Top. A fine interior view of Riverside station in the early 1900s. LNWR loco crews pose proudly by their 'Special Tanks'. It was only a short covered walk from the platforms down a ramp to the floating landing stage and waiting trans-Atlantic liners. Photograph J. Ryan collection.

Middle. Patriot 4-6-0 No 45518 BRADSHAW eases a boat train out of Riverside station and across the swingbridge over the entrance to Princes Dock in July 1955. The signal controlling both railway and maritime traffic is prominent on the left. Although the bridge has been dismantled, the stone abutments are still visible. Photograph J.A. Peden collection.

Bottom. No 49173 returning light engine to Edge Hill after bringing its boat train down to Riverside station on 2nd May 1959. Warehouses serving Princes Half-Tide Dock are prominent behind the loco. The building with the very tall chimney is one of the MD&HB engine sheds, and standing outside is No 16, an Avonside 0-6-0ST dating from 1912. Photograph J.A. Peden.

SPEKE JUNCTION (8C) SHED ALLOCATION JANUARY 1954

Ex-LMS Stanier/English Electric 0-6-0 Diesel Electric: 12003, 12007, 12008, 12011, 12014, 12015, 12016, 12017, 12018, 12020, 12024, 12025, 12026, 12027, 12028

Ex-LMS Hughes/Fowler 5MT 2-6-0: 42786, 42849, 42892

Ex-LMS 3F 0-6-0T: 47284, 47373, 47388, 47439, 47490, 47516, 47651

Ex-LMS Stanier 8F 2-8-0: 48039, 48054, 48094, 48323, 48373, 48502, 48504, 48506, 48511, 48522, 48630, 48631, 48729, 48747

Ex-LNWR/LMS 7F 0-8-0: 48942, 48944, 49134, 49143, 49153, 49155, 49395, 49398, 49406, 49420, 49451

Ex-L&Y Aspinall 2F 0-6-0ST: 51439

Ex-L&Y Aspinall 3F 0-6-0: 52163, 52175, 52438

Total allocation 54

Top. Seen from Picton Road bridge, Jubilee 4-6-0 No 45695 MINOTAUR of Farnley Junction shed approaches with the 9.00am from Hull to Liverpool Lime Street on 12th June 1959. The large building top left was the wagon repair shop, believed to date from Liverpool & Manchester days. Rough shunts and occasional runaways provided plenty of work for this establishment. Note the very long line of vans in the sidings. Photograph J.F. Ward collection.

Middle. A glimpse of the incredibly complex network near Edge Hill shed on 30th March 1968. The elevated signal box is Edge Hill No 4, the high level line to the right of it leading to Engine Shed Junction and the marshalling yards. Stanier 8F 2-8-0 No 48308 has just emerged from the bridge to the left of the box and is about to go through another bridge into the motive power depot. The coaling stage is behind the photographer and the main line to Crewe and London curves sharply away to the left. Photograph J.A. Sommerfield.

Bottom. On 1st April 1968, four months before the end of steam, class 5 4-6-0 No 45231 waits for the road at Engine Shed Junction. The train had come through Allerton and had just left the main line at Wavertree Junction. It was ready to pass round the rear of the engine shed, cross the Manchester line and deposit its load in the lower reception sidings. Hopper wagons on the elevated coaling stage can be seen to the right of the engine. Photograph J.A. Sommerfield.

The west end of Edge Hill shed, showing fourteen of the twenty roads, photographed from the elevated circular goods line on 13th June 1964. Locomotives visible include D217, D3019, 70008 BLACK PRINCE and 42924. Immediately beyond the shed, the Liverpool-Manchester line (in a cutting) is spanned by two girder bridges carrying lines from Spekeland Road sidings near Edge Hill station. The nearer one leads towards Manchester and the one beyond it heads for the Gridiron upper reception sidings. At a higher level still are rows of vans in the marshalling yard. Photograph J.F. Ward.

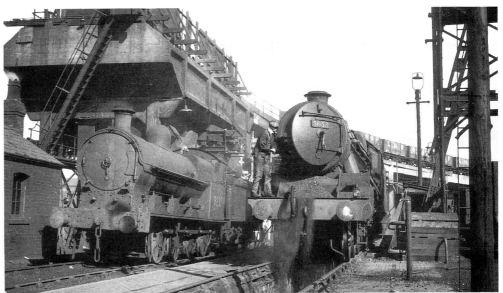

Edge Hill coaling plant in June 1935 with ex-LNWR 0-8-0 No 9211 being refuelled and 'Jubilee' 4-6-0 No 5652 HAWKE having its smokebox emptied. One of the 'Loco' coal wagons is still lettered LNWR, twelve years after grouping. This unique elevated concrete structure dated from 1914 and was supplied with coal trucks propelled along a 150 yards spur from the elevated goods line near Wavertree Junction. A thousand tons of coal could be delivered to the plant in a day. Photograph W. Potter.

Left. The less glamorous side of railway work 1: Liverpool housewives in heavy overalls enjoy a rest from sweeping out coaches at Edge Hill carriage depot on 19th May 1954. Despite a lick of paint, the staff amenity block was very basic and a shade for the bare light bulb was clearly beyond BR's resources. A ginger tom snoozes on the bench between bouts of tracking down rats in the sidings and sheds. Right. The less glamorous side of railway work 2: clerks with rolled up sleeves and loosened ties pore over ledgers in the former booking office of Alexandra Dock passenger station on 22nd August 1955. Once-fine woodwork, dating from LNWR days, is still evident, but generally the place is a mess of clutter. A lengthy and no doubt ponderous LMS notice about weighbridges and weighing machines is peeling away from the notice board.

Lancashire & Yorkshire System in Liverpool

To Ormskirk and Preston

Scale
0 ¼ ½ ¾ 1   2 miles

To Southport

N

Goods

Maghull

To Southport

To Kirkby and Wigan

Hall Road
Electric Car Sheds

Old Roan

Southport Jn.   *Aintree Jn.*

Blundellsands & Crosby
Goods

British Enka

Fazakerley Sidings

Bridle Road Industrial Estate

Sefton Jn.   Gds

Fazakerley Jn.

Waterloo
Goods

Tar Distillery

Ford

a   b

Aintree Sefton Arms

c   d

Fazakerley

Sidings

Aintree Sorting Sdgs.

Aintree Racecourse

Seaforth & Litherland
Seaforth Jn.

Linacre Road
North Mersey Branch Jn.

a Aintree Loco Shed

Rimrose Road Jns.

Orrell Park

Hartleys Jams

b Aintree Station Jn.

LOR

Marsh Lane Jn.

c Railway Signal Works

d Carriage & Wagon Works

Gladstone Dock

Walton Junction

Preston Road

North Mersey Goods

Goods

Gds.

1 Bootle Village

Marsh Lane & Strand Road

Walton Jn.

2 Millers Bridge

1

Bootle Oriel Road

Kirkdale No. 1 Tunnel

River Mersey

2

LNW Jn.

Kirkdale No. 2 Tunnel

Bootle Jn.

To Halewood

New Brighton

f

Kirkdale

Bankfield Goods

e

Bank Hall

To Edge Hill

g

Bank Hall Loco Sheds

Sandhills Jn.

e Bank Hall Jn.

Sandhills

f Kirkdale Carriage Sdgs.

High Level Coal Railway   h

g Sandhills Sidings

h Regent Road Lift Bridge

North Docks Goods

Exchange Station Jn.

Note: The purpose of this map is to show the location of features rather than the system at a specific period. Therefore, not all stations, depots and installations existed at the same time.

To Edge Hill

Liverpool Exchange

Great Howard Street Goods

━━━ Lancashire & Yorkshire Railway

─·─·─ London & North Western Railway

········· Cheshire Lines Committee Railway

┤┼┼┼├ Liverpool Overhead Railway

┤┼┼┼├ Mersey Docks & Harbour Board Line

Birkenhead

© Paul Anderson 1996

36

CHAPTER 2

LANCASHIRE & YORKSHIRE

With a beaming driver, very smart class 5 4-6-0 No 45207 of Low Moor shed started a Bradford Exchange express out of Liverpool Exchange on 4th April 1953. Photograph S Creer.

It is quite remarkable that one railway enjoyed a monopoly in Liverpool for nearly twenty years. The Liverpool & Manchester and its feeders managed to tap virtually all the coal mining areas and mill towns which relied on the port, although this was by a somewhat indirect route in many instances. Several rival lines were discussed, but the schemes foundered and the only competition of sorts was at Birkenhead, over in the Wirral. A certain amount of complacency set in; during 1838, for example, Liverpool & Manchester carriages were described as 'glorified pig pens'. This situation was bound to change with the eruption of railway promotion during the 'mania' years of 1844-45. The outcome was three new lines from the north and east of Liverpool which converged before they reached the town, then ran into a terminus close to the main commercial district. Opening of the system took place in stages from 1848 to 1850.

Initially, by far the most important route was that from Bury, which provided a real alternative to the Liverpool & Manchester as far as the Lancashire coalfield, Manchester and West Yorkshire were concerned. A second line came in from Preston and eventually formed the principal route from Liverpool to Carlisle and Scotland. The third railway began as a decidedly country branch from the village of Southport, but in time became the busiest of all in terms of residential traffic. These three lines should have formed a

Tithebarn Street station.
Drawing by Juliet Whitworth.

cohesive system, bonded in competition with the LNWR, but suspicion and squabbling created a rather shambolic alliance. In due course they all came together under the Lancashire & Yorkshire Railway. This hardly improved matters and by the mid-1870s the L&Y had gained an unenviable reputation as the most inefficient railway in the country. Sheer determination supported by a rapidly growing income transformed the company into one of the best in England by 1890. Locomotive engineer Barton Wright furnished the line with a stud of sturdy reliable engines,

Sandhills station on 9th March 1957, looking north towards Walton Junction. Stanier 4MT 2-6-4T No 42620 of Accrington shed (24A) rolls through with an express, probably from the Blackburn and Burnley direction. LMS electric stock is on the left, whilst Sandhills No 2 box can be seen in the distance. Photograph J A Peden collection.

A grim prospect of Sandhills station subway on 25th March 1958, with water leaks everywhere and the glazed brick facing cracked and sagging. The booking office and barrier in the background were housed in a timber building half way up the embankment. Stairs to the island platform, now the only passenger access, are in the centre.

Smoke from Bank Hall shed drifts across Stanley Road on 24th March 1954. The line from Exchange to Walton Junction is in the foreground, whilst the Southport tracks curve away on the left. This view from Commercial Road shows the street frontage of Bank Hall station in the left background, the tramway overhead on Stanley Road and the shed coaling tower in the distance.

The newer No 2 shed at Bank Hall Motive Power Depot (27A) on 13th October 1957. Three ex-L&Y 0-4-0ST 'Pugs', Nos 51232, 51206 and 51229 rest between duties on the dock lines. Photograph J A Peden collection.

passenger services were smartened up, and goods facilities underwent a massive expansion. On Merseyside the approach tracks were quadrupled, Exchange terminus was rebuilt, and freight operations were centred on the vast marshalling yard at Aintree.

Although the L&Y was confined to the northern half of Liverpool, it captured more than its fair share of goods and passenger traffic. For a start, the company was well placed to exploit the expansion of the port towards Bootle, five large depots eventually serving the docks. Suburban housing spread northwards as well, bordering the three lines for several miles. Commuter traffic burgeoned and pioneering electrification schemes were implemented during Edwardian years. A bonus came from leisure traffic. Aintree racecourse was next to the Preston line, but income from Grand National specials was confined to one hectic weekend a year. Southport was a different matter. Besides providing regular residential business, the town developed into a popular holiday resort, especially for day trippers. Although shorn of their expresses, the ex-L&Y lines in Liverpool still carry frequent and heavily used local services.

FROM BURY AND PRESTON

Inspiration for the Bury line did not originate in Liverpool, but came from businessmen in Bolton and Wigan, intent on breaking the Liverpool & Manchester monopoly. The idea was first mooted in 1844, the extension to Bury being agreed in 1845. Despite fierce opposition from the Liverpool & Manchester company, the Liverpool & Bury Railway obtained its Act of Parliament for a line from Bury to Borough Gaol in Liverpool on 31st July 1845. But with hostility unabated, the Bury proprietors sought an ally in the form of the Manchester & Leeds Railway. This concern was no stranger to aggressive rivals, having opened its line across the Pennines in 1839-41 after a decade of opposition from landowners and canal interests. The Manchester & Leeds was very enthusiastic about an outlet to the Mersey and absorbed the Liverpool & Bury on 27th July 1846, a line from Rochdale to Bury providing the connection. Just over three weeks earlier the smaller company had gained parliamentary approval for an extension from Borough Gaol to Tithebarn Street nearer the centre of Liverpool. The Manchester & Leeds changed its title to the grander sounding Lancashire & Yorkshire Railway by an Act dated 9th July 1847.

Meanwhile another local company was going through a similar sequence of enthusiastic promotion, tough opposition and then seeking protection from an established neighbour. The Liverpool, Ormskirk & Preston Railway also issued its prospectus in 1844. Its first attempt to obtain parliamentary approval failed

Kirkdale station, looking north through Westminster Road bridge to Kirkdale East signal box and the cutting leading to Kirkdale No 2 tunnel. The electrified Ormskirk tracks are in the foreground, whilst the fast lines, lifted by the time this view was taken, were beyond the far platform. This was a very complex railway site, with the CLC Huskisson branch in a deep cutting off to the right and the LNWR Bootle branch passing beneath the station behind the camera. Photograph J F Ward collection.

in 1845 because of opposition from other railways, the proposed branch from Ormskirk to Southport reluctantly being abandoned as a result. In the next session, the Liverpool, Ormskirk & Preston was successful and acquired its Act on 16th August 1846. In this case support came from the East Lancashire Railway which had been formed in 1844 with the amalgamation of two local companies created to link the cotton towns of Blackburn, Accrington, Burnley, Colne, Rawtenstall and Bury with Manchester. The Blackburn & Preston Railway was absorbed in 1846. There had been strong backing for the Liverpool, Ormskirk & Preston by the East Lancashire from the outset, and a clause in its Act sanctioned amalgamation, if mutually agreed. This duly took place in October 1846.

There had been conflict between the East Lancashire and Manchester & Leeds from the outset, hostilities continuing in early Lancashire & Yorkshire days. This acrimony extended to their respective Liverpool satellites, but at least there was a sensible decision to build the line from Walton to Great Howard Street jointly. Construction work on the Bury route began early in 1846 and involved hefty expenditure on tunnels, viaducts and earthworks. From a tunnel through the ridge at Orrell, west of Wigan, the line dropped steadily from 300 feet at gradients of up to 1 in 100. Work on the Preston line began in March 1847, involving a less elevated passage across marshland and gently undulating ground. There were some level sections, but also gradients up to 1 in 132 - although most were considerably gentler. After dropping to a mere 25 feet above sea level near Rufford, the line climbed to 150 feet at Ormskirk before descending to Maghull.

The railways gradually converged and were within two miles of each other about seven miles from the centre of Liverpool. The Bury line passed through Kirkby, about 80 feet above the Mersey, crossed the River Alt, then rose slightly to Fazakerley before reaching Walton Junction. From Maghull at 70 feet, the Preston tracks dipped across the Alt valley then rose through Aintree prior to a slight downhill stretch to 80 feet at Walton Junction.

LIVER BIRD

One of the most expensive sections of the Bury and Preston system was the joint line to Great Howard Street. Like the Liverpool & Manchester, it was faced with the sandstone ridge, and south of Walton Junction the tracks were soon in a deep cutting through the red rock. Then came Kirkdale No 1 and No 2 tunnels through Breeze Hill, 498 yards and 210 yards respectively, with a 111 yard sheer-walled gap between them. The line continued to fall at 1 in 276 then 1 in 453 through these excavations. Another deep cutting took the railway to Hawthorne Road in Kirkdale. Half of the steady two mile descent to Great Howard Street was

on a 30 feet high viaduct comprising 117 brick arches made up of 26 million bricks. As the port spread northwards, this lofty passage gave a good view of docks, warehouses and associated industry.

The Liverpool & Bury line opened to passenger traffic on 20th November 1848, its double track route having cost nearly £1 million. Goods traffic commenced a month later because of delays in the completion of facilities at Great Howard Street. Trains began running on the Preston line, also double track, on 2nd April 1849. In the Liverpool area seven stations were provided at first. Bootle Lane on the joint line, about two miles from Great Howard Street, was renamed Kirkdale in 1876. The Bury line had Preston Road (3 miles), Simonswood (4.5 miles) and Kirkby (6.5 miles). Simonswood was renamed Aintree around 1849 and became Fazakerley in March 1860. The Preston line had Walton Junction (3 miles), Aintree (4.25 miles) and Maghull (6.75 miles). North Docks station was added to the joint line in June 1854. It stood just under a mile south of Bootle Lane and was renamed Sandhills in 1857.

Station buildings were rather dull affairs, mainly in red brick and displaying a mere hint of the classical styling still popular on contemporary lines elsewhere. Great Howard Street (ominously known as Borough Gaol in Lancashire & Yorkshire rather than East Lancashire timetables) was very basic, for it was only intended to be a temporary terminus. Intermediate stations have been modified or extended and eventually rationalised over the ensuing years. At Kirkdale a plain brick structure still exists at street level, whilst the timber booking office, half way up the side of the embankment, remains at Sandhills. Great Howard Street was eliminated as the passenger terminus when the extension to Tithebarn Street (Exchange) opened in 1850 (see later).

With the opening of the Bury line, the L&Y could compete with the LNWR for Liverpool-Manchester traffic. It also had a through route from Merseyside to the West Riding and the east coast at Goole. Several Lancashire cotton towns and villages also benefited from much better communications with the Mersey docks. Despite an inconvenient reversal at Lostock Hall, the journey time between Preston and Liverpool was cut to less than an hour, a considerable improvement on the LNWR route via Earlestown and Wigan. The Ormskirk line also became an important artery for through trains to Blackpool and Glasgow. Freight traffic reached enormous proportions, particularly on the Bury line, once goods depots and dock branches were established (see last section). Coal and cotton inevitably formed a large proportion of the business.

The long-standing feud between the East Lancashire and L&Y finally ended on 13th August 1859 when the former was absorbed by the latter. Nevertheless the East Lancashire engines with their copper capped chimneys and polished brass domes were around for some time. As part of the massive L&Y improvement programme the joint line from Liverpool to Walton Junction was quadrupled in the 1880s, involving new tunnels parallel to the originals at Kirkdale. The impressive 1848 portals were authentically duplicated and, despite widening, the sandstone cuttings remained awesome excavations.

As Liverpool's suburbs expanded, commuter traffic increased substantially. In Edwardian years the L&Y embarked on an ambitious and pioneering electrification scheme based on Exchange station. The initial route to Southport was inaugurated on 22nd March 1904 and proved an overwhelming success, so the new form of traction was introduced on the Ormskirk line. Electric trains from Sandhills Junction served Aintree from 3rd December 1906 and Maghull from 1st October 1909, eventually reaching Ormskirk on 1st April 1913. Orrell Park station, less than half a mile north of Walton Junction, opened in 1906 to coincide with electrification to Aintree. It had fairly generous side platforms, but the booking office adjacent to Orrell Lane bridge, together with the waiting shelters, were basic timber structures. Old Roan Halt, actually better placed to serve Aintree village, opened in May 1907 when

a steam rail-motor shuttle was introduced between Aintree and Ormskirk. It closed on 1st October 1909 when electric multiple units began working to Maghull. A new station was provided on the same site during 1933 to serve new housing developments, and it proved much more durable.

Rationalisation began in the 1960s with the withdrawal of local goods facilities. Maghull yard closed on 7th September 1964, followed by Preston Road on 7th December 1964, Aintree on 8th February 1965 and Kirkby on 4th December 1965. Sandhills survived until 4th November 1974. Merseyrail developments in the centre of Liverpool had suburban repercussions on the old L&Y routes, principally electrification to Kirkby on 2nd May 1977. However, through trains on the Preston and Bury routes ceased (the former somewhat earlier); both Ormskirk and Kirkby now function as the terminus for frequent suburban services, with comparatively sparse onward connections provided by dmus. For those fascinated by timetables, it would be an interesting exercise to work out the quickest rail journey from one end of Ormskirk station to the other!

THE SOUTHPORT LINE

In 1840 Southport was still a village, although it had already been frequented by bathers for some time. Further south, the stretch of sandy shoreline around Bootle had also been discovered by pleasure seekers, and a few wealthy merchants had

built houses there. Clearly there was some potential for a railway along the coast, but the Bill for a Liverpool - Southport - Preston line was rejected by parliament in 1846. A more modest proposal came in the form of the Liverpool, Crosby & Southport Railway which was successful and obtained its Act on 2nd July 1847. It comprised a 12.75 mile branch from the Bury/Preston line near Bootle Lane, about a mile and a half north of the proposed Tithebarn Street terminus.

Construction work began during March 1848 and proceeded remarkably quickly, the line as far south as Waterloo being ready by June 1848. Most of the trackbed lay on the landward side of a long stretch of sand dunes, the only structural work of any note being a small bridge over the River Alt. Just one line of rails was laid at first, although the formation could accommodate double track. The cost had been a mere £40,000. A modest service of five trains each way between Southport and Waterloo began on 21st July 1848, passengers being conveyed to and from Liverpool by horse bus.

Unfortunately the company soon ran into financial difficulties and work on the connection to the joint line was postponed. However, this link was clearly vital to the Liverpool, Crosby & Southport's future prospects, so construction resumed in February 1850. This section required a fair amount of embankment, together with several bridges, including one over the Leeds & Liverpool canal. Southport

Fairburn 2-6-4T No 42279, carrying express headcode, rushes through Preston Road station with a train consisting of four non-corridor coaches bound for Liverpool Exchange on 20th March 1957. The goods yard had facilities for household coal to the right and general merchandise near the platforms, horse-drawn carts and motor vehicles for local deliveries being in evidence. The overbridge carries the main road to Preston, hence the original name of the station, but the more appropriate local designation Rice Lane now appears on the platform signs. Photograph J A Peden collection.

Fazakerley station had a fairly basic main building, the predominant red brick livened up with cream brick headers for the door and window openings. This view, looking north, was probably taken before World War 1. Photograph J Ryan collection.

Walton Junction station on 30th May 1960, looking north towards Aintree. Ex-LMS 2P 4-4-0 No 40684 pilots Standard 4MT 4-6-0 No 75049, both of Bank Hall shed, with a Blackpool North - Liverpool Exchange train. Photograph F Dean, J F Ward collection.

Orrell Park station was built in 1906 to serve suburban development around the convergence of Moss Lane, Orrell Lane and Rice Lane north of Walton. This L&Y investment stemmed from the success of the Ormskirk electrification and was clearly justified, for the station is still open. Painting was taking place in this Edwardian view. Photograph J Ryan collection.

trains finally began running through to Tithebarn Street (Exchange) and were hauled by L&Y engines. Once completed, the line proved to be a huge success and suburban traffic between Liverpool and Crosby soon became too much for the single track. Doubling of this section was completed on 1st June 1852, the remaining stretch to Southport following three months later. There were endless quarrels about tolls for the use of the joint line and the L&Y, showing a certain amount of contempt for its less powerful neighbour, absorbed the Liverpool, Crosby & Southport without consultation on 1st January 1855. This had, however, been authorised in principle by parliament back in August 1850. The outcome was even more friction between the East Lancashire and L&Y. When the Manchester & Southport Railway opened in April 1855, the East Lancashire began to operate a Liverpool - Southport service via a spur at Burscough and a price war flared up.

Waterloo was just five and a quarter miles from Tithebarn Street/Exchange, but at one time or another there were no less than seven intermediate stations (including Sandhills on the joint line). Four of them opened at various dates in October, November and December 1850 - Millers Bridge (two and a half miles from Tithebarn Street), Bootle Village (3 miles), Marsh Lane (3.25 miles), and Seaforth (4.25 miles). Bank Hall, two miles from Exchange, joined them in 1870. A new Bootle station, mid-way between Bootle Village and Millers Bridge, opened in 1876, its neighbours closing as a result. Marsh Lane was rebuilt on a slightly different site in 1886 and renamed Marsh Lane and Strand Road. That completed the pattern of stations still open today, but there were three name changes over the years. Seaforth became Seaforth & Litherland in 1905; Bootle was altered to Bootle Oriel Road during 1924; Marsh Lane & Strand Road became Bootle New Strand in 1967.

Early station buildings on the Southport line were brick structures characterised by hipped roofs and prominent eaves. The two storey versions were tall and quite impressive in their own way, but very little money was spent on embellishments. From Seaforth southwards all traces of Liverpool, Crosby & Southport architecture was swept away by closures and quadrupling during the 1880s. Standard L&Y buildings featuring big gabled canopies then became the norm. Bank Hall had a bleak brick booking office on the overbridge, Bootle Oriel Road was provided with equally austere facilities facing the street, and Waterloo gained a large yet dull station in 1881 when the level crossing was replaced by a bridge.

Apart from the underground Mersey Railway (Chapter 4), by late Victorian times the Southport line had become the busiest commuter route into Liverpool. The steam service of around 40 trains each way a day was proving unsatisfactory, thus the decision to electrify. The first electric trains ran on 22nd March 1904 and the improvement was spectacular. By the summer there were 63 trains from Exchange to Southport on weekdays, plus 12 expresses stopping only at Birkdale, and no less than 56 locals to Hall Road on the northern edge of Crosby. Slotting in with these were the steam-hauled Euston - Southport through coaches mentioned in Chapter 1. In later years, when these had been replaced by Southport - Lime Street dmus, unsuspecting passengers wondered why they were being treated to a tour of the Edge Hill complex en route!

A frequent electric service has been operating on the Southport line for nearly a century, with just two changes of rolling stock. In many ways the line has altered little, although there have been modifications to the nature of the workings and a couple of traumatic episodes. World War Two brought considerable disruption including the complete destruction of Marsh Lane & Strand Road station which was closed from 19th May 1941 to 12th July 1943. The locals to Bank Hall were also permanently withdrawn during the conflict. Local freight has never been important, the only yard of any size at Marsh Lane closing on 30th April 1973. However, Beeching recommended closure of the whole line in 1963. This ludicrous idea was quickly over-ruled, and looking at the well-used six-coach trains running every 15 minutes today, it is incredible to think that pure profit and loss considerations might have triumphed over common-sense three decades ago. In 1995 there were 71 trains from Liverpool to Southport on weekdays, all of them stopping at all stations.

EXCHANGE

Although Borough Gaol (Great Howard Street) was the terminus stipulated by the original Liverpool & Bury Act, the company soon approached parliament for authority to build an extension, just over a quarter of a mile, to Tithebarn Street. This duly received its Act, on 3rd August 1846, and work began in January 1849. The East Lancashire subscribed half the cost, but the L&Y insisted on having its own way with virtually every aspect of the layout and design of the new terminus. As early as February 1849, the East Lancashire considered building its own station, but clearly could not afford it. The subsequent uneasy co-habitation was reflected in dual identity - Tithebarn Street to the East Lancashire and Exchange as far as the L&Y was concerned.

The extension began just south of a brick arch over the LNWR Waterloo branch, then curved fairly sharply round the eastern wall of Borough Gaol. After

A train of L&Y electric stock arriving at Maghull on an Ormskirk-Liverpool Exchange working in the 1930s. These pioneering trains were replaced by the LMS between 1939 and 1942. Photograph J A Peden collection.

The exterior of Bootle Oriel Road station, looking south, on 19th November 1952. By this time the 1876 buildings were becoming somewhat ramshackle and a new entrance block was provided in 1953. Note the Liverpool Corporation bus and the none too prestigious headquarters of the *Bootle Times*!

Marsh Lane & Strand Road station was destroyed in May 1941 during the blitz. It reopened in July 1943 without buildings, which were finally provided in 1945. M28353M heads a Southport-Liverpool Exchange train in the late 1950s. The Midland Langton Dock branch tunnels beneath the L&Y at this point.

crossing the Leeds & Liverpool canal by a lattice iron bridge, the track climbed at 1 in 84, then 1 in 94 to the terminus some 25 feet above Tithebarn Street. It was built entirely on brick arches forming an undercroft and involved the demolition of 540 houses, most of which were abysmal slums. The station opened on 13th May 1850; a notable piece of architecture, its frontage reflected the powerful dignity which railway companies were attempting to portray at the time, and its overall roof was a radical piece of design.

John Hawkshaw designed the buildings and excelled with the two storey facade, a particularly fine example of contemporary 'Railway Italianate'. Well proportioned at 120 feet wide and 90 feet height, it had an arched entrance in the centre, pedimented windows in ashlar (smooth stone) on the first floor, and round headed windows in rusticated (rough hewn) stone on the ground floor. A staircase with balustrades led up to the plinth on which the station stood, and solemn pillars marked the driveway entrance from Tithebarn Street.

ROMAN CATHOLIC CATHEDRAL

Behind the main building two amenity wings extended for nearly 200 feet parallel to the tracks. Between them were five platforms, one for arrivals and two each for L&Y and East Lancashire departures. The partners also had their own booking offices, refreshment rooms and waiting rooms. Most of the station was sheltered by asymmetrical gabled train sheds, the smaller one 78 feet wide and the larger one tapering from 136 feet at its broadest point. The roof took six months to erect and was very advanced for its time, being the first to be constructed entirely of iron and glass.

Great Howard Street station was substantially expanded as a goods depot while work proceeded on the Tithebarn Street extension. Matters were complicated by the LNWR Waterloo branch which passed immediately north of the site at a low level and was being built at the same time. The approach to Great Howard Street depot and the beginning of the Tithebarn Street line, a total of eleven tracks, were carried across the North Western on a huge 60 feet high

Seaforth & Litherland station on 29th August 1955 with a Liverpool Overhead Railway train in what was then the bay platform. There was formerly another platform on the extreme left, but this was destroyed in an air raid. Photograph T J Edgington.

brick arch with a 150 feet span. Wedge shaped in plan, it was 200 feet wide at the southern end and bore oval stone plaques, one stating 'John Hawkshaw Engineer 1849' and another depicting a Liver Bird. Just to the east, a second 150 feet span across the LNWR (this time in cast iron) carried tracks into a new yard on the northern edge of the complex. Further expansion was possible when Borough Gaol closed in 1855 and the L&Y leased the land three years later for its own purposes.

Tithebarn Street station, by then always known as Exchange, was proving woefully inadequate as the 1870s dawned. In twenty years its five platforms had come to accommodate increasing amounts of residential, intermediate and long distance traffic. Widening of the approach viaduct to four tracks and an expansion of the station on its eastern side were sanctioned in 1876, but the results of a competition to design the new facade were described as 'ugly'. No work was done and congestion became acute. By 1882 reconstruction of the station and its approaches on an altogether more massive scale was being contemplated in the L&Y boardroom. The way for this was cleared when Liverpool Corporation agreed to certain street closures and the Leeds & Liverpool canal was persuaded to divert its waterway into a new basin. An Act of 24th July 1882 authorised a separate four-track approach line from Exchange Station

A corner of Great Howard Street goods station on 12th November 1960 with Bank Hall 'Pug' No 51206 on shunting duty. The line into Exchange ran on the viaduct to the left. Massive dock warehouses form a backdrop. Photograph J F Ward.

Junction, avoiding curves which still veered round the long vanished Borough Gaol, whilst another Act of 2nd August 1883 sanctioned a new terminus, virtually at street level.

The approach line extended for nearly three quarters of a mile and was entirely on a viaduct of red sandstone arches, plate girders across streets, and deck girders on columns in Great Howard Street yard. Steel lattice spans carried the rails across the Waterloo branch at a high level, directly above the 1849 cast iron spans mentioned earlier. The line from Exchange Station Junction opened on 12th December 1886, together with the first part of the terminus, resulting in the closure and demolition of Hawkshaw's building. On 2nd July 1888 the remainder of the station was brought into use

and the problem of coping with L&Y passenger traffic in Liverpool had been solved.

In its final form Exchange had ten platform faces, all but two of them extending for about 200 yards. They were numbered 1 to 10 from east to west, No 1 being considerably shorter and adapted to deal with inward parcels traffic. A cab road ran between Nos 3 and 4. The site was enclosed by massive brick walls bordering Pall Mall and East Street, the intervening areas sheltered by a light and lofty overall roof. Appropriately, the great train shed at Liverpool Street station in London seems to have provided the inspiration. The Exchange version displayed less aesthetic quality, but nevertheless it was pleasing to the eye. There were actually four longitudinal gabled roofs, three

Above. The exterior of Liverpool Exchange station in Tithebarn Street on 16th April 1977. Surmounting the archways either side of the rather fine clock are busts of King Edward VII and Queen Alexandra. Below the clock is a bust of John Pearson, chairman of the Lancashire & Yorkshire Railway from 1883 until his death in 1887. Photograph J F Ward.

Right. The cab circulating area at Liverpool Exchange was generous to say the least, as clearly shown by this view taken on 2nd June 1950. Exchange Hotel is on the left and the concourse amenities block to the right. A splendid taxi of 1920s vintage waits for passengers whilst Simpson's shop in the corner urges people to buy binoculars and barometers. Exchange had early examples of proper shops - rather than kiosks - situated within a station. Elsewhere, there was a poster for a shop in Rodney Street proclaiming, 'We can still measure, make and fit a Brook's Rupture Appliance in one visit!'

Bottom right. On the concourse of Exchange all manner of clutter offered services to passengers. There were five rather ramshackle telephone booths, the inevitable W H Smith bookstall, a Ray & Miles furniture showroom, and a small Cunard/White Star kiosk. Finlay's tobacco stall advertised the pleasures of Abdulla cigarettes and an 'I speak your weight' machine stood near one of those wonderful contraptions which stamped metal name tags. At 3.52pm on 2nd June 1950 a GPO Morris Commercial van waited for mail off the trains.

The entrance to platforms 5 and 6 at Exchange on 2nd June 1950, with non-corridor trains for other parts of Lancashire awaiting departure time. That at platform 4 was double headed by an Ivatt mogul and a 2-6-4T. One of the posters advertised a week in Bonnie Scotland for £15-15s, inclusive of rail fare, accommodation, sightseeing trips, reserved seats, meals on trains and gratuities!

By 17th August 1969 Exchange was already looking very run down, although closure was nearly eight years away. This view looking out from platform 4 shows No 2 box and parts of Great Howard Street goods station. Photograph J A Sommerfield.

broad ones and a narrower, more steeply pitched version over platforms 4 and 5. Slender columns, devoid of decoration yet very elegant, supported the structure. In total, the shed covered 23,600 square yards and cost £285,000.

An amenity block behind the concourse contained the outward parcels office, refreshment rooms and waiting rooms. This self-contained building actually stood beneath the train shed and was clad in yellow glazed tiles with dark green relief. Kiosks behind the buffer stops contained left luggage, enquiry and booking offices, finished off with neat cabinet work in dark and light tints. A cab yard with a transverse glazed roof stood between the amenity block and Exchange Hotel, the latter in effect the public face of the station. The 1880s saw railway architecture at its lowest ebb in many ways. Rather than trying to impress the public, as at the original Tithebarn Street terminus, companies were trying to outdo each other, and some massive but ungainly buildings resulted. Exchange Hotel was a huge edifice in 'Free Renaissance' style, the bulky central section and rather apologetic *porte cochere* in front of the hotel entrance being out of proportion with the rest of the facade. Still, it did have some redeeming features, such as well-executed columns flanking the windows and a magnificent projecting clock. The hotel, which opened on 13th August 1888 and contained 150 bedrooms, a ballroom and a banqueting hall, certainly made an impact on Tithebarn Street.

At first Exchange station had plenty of spare capacity; in 1888 there were 115 trains into the terminus on weekdays and about the same number of departures. Traffic was controlled by two signal boxes, one with 168 levers and the other with 136. The number of services increased substantially after electrification to Southport, Aintree and Ormskirk, and the station stimulated business in the northern part of Liverpool city centre. Some 300 staff were employed at Exchange.

The L&Y and LNWR merged on 1st January 1922, and the resulting giant became part of the LMS group on 1st January 1923. Until World War 2 there were few changes, although the 40 minute expresses between Liverpool and Manches-

The Exchange approaches, looking north away from the terminus, possibly in 1950. No 1 box spans a siding to the right and its imposing gantry frames a number of interesting features. On the left, the course of the original 1850 approach line comes in through a gap in the 1886 viaduct parapet. In the centre, part of Great Howard Street depot towers above the hefty girder bridge over the LNWR Waterloo branch. On the right, part of the huge Don Corn Mills off Chadwick Street peers through the mist. Out of sight, a maze of sidings wandered below the main line tracks.

The approach to Exchange, looking south towards the terminus, possibly in 1950. No 2 box can be seen in the distance, its gantry sporting eleven posts with 22 arms, including stubby signals for shunting movements. The four train sheds, with their seemingly odd alignment determined by the existing road layout, stretch away towards Tithebarn Street. Gable ends of gutted warehouses between Pall Mall and the Leeds & Liverpool canal basin rear up on the left. Note the short lengths of conductor rail between the maze of points.

ter were retimed at 45 minutes to ease locomotive work with heavy trains over the stiff gradients. In 1929 there were eleven such workings on weekdays, departing from Exchange between 8.35am and 8.40pm. Most continued beyond Manchester Victoria to Leeds, Bradford or York. There was a restaurant car express to Newcastle and through coaches to Hull Riverside for the Zeebrugge steamer in summer. Slower trains went via Wigan and Bolton, whilst others veered off to Rochdale and beyond.

On the East Lancashire route, the earliest train was the 1.50am to Preston which connected with overnight Scottish expresses. In daytime there were fast trains to Blackpool Talbot Road, Blackpool Central and Carlisle. Through carriages went to Windermere and Whitehaven, and a restaurant car express departed for Glasgow and Edinburgh. Prior to World War 1 certain Scottish trains had been hauled by Midland locos all the way from Liverpool. Most locals finished at Preston but some continued to Accrington, Burnley and Colne. Long distance workings mainly used platforms 2 to 6 at Exchange.

Local electric trains were accommodated at platforms 7 to 10, these being equipped with electric rather than traditional board indicators. Although intervals were not absolutely precise, there was basically a 10 minute service to Hall Road,

alternate workings continuing to Southport Chapel Street. Trains left for Ormskirk at roughly 20 minute intervals, with additional workings terminating at Aintree. Some of these travelled via Linacre Road (see next section).

Southport services were considerably augmented during holiday periods and several non-stop 30 minute expresses ran. On August Bank Holiday Monday in 1929 there were no less than nine departures between 12 noon and 1.00pm. Grand National day during the same year saw a virtually continuous service to Aintree, when as many as 33,000 people were moved out and back. Fifty trains left Exchange between 10.30am and 2.30pm, and an astonishing 36 trains returned in two and a half hours - a train every four minutes!

The blitz affected Liverpool Exchange badly. A large part of the roof over platforms 9 and 10 was destroyed in one raid, whilst two piers and three spans of the approach viaduct collapsed in another attack. This blockage lasted three months. Approximately 100 steam and 250 electric trains carrying 70,000 passengers used Exchange on weekdays prior to World War Two, but the station had had its best days by then. Eventually long distance and non-electrified local services began to decline or were diverted into Lime Street. Great Howard Street goods closed on 30th September 1963. At the same time the terminus itself took on a

woebegone and neglected air, though the Southport, Ormskirk and Kirkby trains were still heavily used, and in the 1970s a bold plan was formulated to take these further into the city centre, providing convenient connections with both the Wirral electrics and main line services at Lime Street.

A major element in this scheme was the Liverpool Loop (see Chapter 4) but as far as the former L&Y system was concerned the principal work was a new tunnel from the former Great Howard Street alignment to Central Low Level. Exchange station closed on 2nd May 1977 and two days later trains began to use the new route, an underground station at Moorfields catering for the area around Tithebarn Street. The former hotel frontage has been retained and incorporated in a massive office, shop and entertainment complex occupying the site of the ten platforms. From a Northern Line electric the remains of the 1886 approach viaduct can still be seen, a poignant reminder of the great days.

THE DOCK BRANCHES

Although the three radial L&Y routes out of Liverpool are still intact, several once incredibly busy dock lines have met the same fate as Exchange. In addition to Great Howard Street, the company built five main depots to serve the port. Three of them were served directly by L&Y branches, with access to the other two over MD&HB tracks. Among the prolific traffic, bales of imported cotton and coal for export or ship's bunkers reflected the significance of the Lancashire hinterland, although machinery destined for all over the world and foodstuffs to satisfy Britain's appetite were important as well. The branches involved some interesting engineering works; one of them also boasted Aintree yard and shed, a racecourse station, and an electric suburban service.

The Liverpool, Ormskirk & Preston Act of 1846 authorised a branch from Kirkdale to the docks and when the L&Y was formed in 1847 this proposed line became joint property. Although North Docks goods depot opened in 1848, nothing was done about the branch and powers lapsed. By 1850 Lancashire collieries were sending over 400,000 tons of coal to Liverpool, and a deputation of mine owners asked the dock authorities to build the line. There was agreement, indeed enthusiasm, for this 'High Level Coal Railway' but again no progress was made. Eventually the L&Y made a move and on 2nd June 1854 obtained an Act for a three quarter mile branch from the joint line at North Docks station to North Docks goods depot, together with newly opened Wellington, Sandon, Nelson and Stanley Docks.

From Sandhills Junction the single track dropped at 1 in 400, then 1 in 240 and finally 1 in 108 on a brick viaduct punctuated by plate girder bridges over Holme Street, Errington Street and Grundy Street. After crossing Great Howard Street the line split into two branches. That on the left descended for 170 yards and entered North Docks depot at street level, the first goods moving by rail on 26th March 1855. From here, sidings later taken over by the MD&HB ran along Regent Road to various docks. The right hand spur crossed Regent Road to reach high level drops alongside Wellington Dock, enabling coal to be discharged directly into ships. Wagons began to move over the High Level Coal Railway on 23rd December 1856 and eventually 4,000 tons of fuel a day was handled by the quayside hydraulic machinery.

The span across Regent Road was a vertical lift bridge designed to rise 8 feet, enabling large loads to be moved along the dock road. It was also very ugly, the

Ex-L&Y 0-4-0ST No 51206 posing against the rather grotesque lift bridge carrying the High Level Coal Railway across Regent Road on 9th May 1959. The 'Pug' is actually standing directly above the point where the Liverpool Overhead Railway descended to street level to pass beneath this L&Y branch. Bank Hall's 'Pugs' were more used to working below the LOR and were thus equipped with a swivelling spark deflector which can be seen clearly. Photograph J A Peden.

Middle right. Bankfield Goods, looking east towards Derby Road on 11th April 1959. Former L&Y Aspinall 0-6-0T No 51537 was a regular performer in the yard. Built in 1897 and withdrawn in 1961, it was the very last ex-LMS loco to receive its BR number. Photograph J B Horne.

Bottom right. Hughes/Fowler 'Crab' 2-6-0 No 42878 in a corner of Bankfield Goods Depot on 10th August 1963. Elder Dempster Lines freighter APAPA berthed at Canada Dock can be seen in the background. Photograph J A Sommerfield.

Aintree Sorting Sidings East box on the North Mersey branch, looking towards Kirkby, 24th April 1957. Aintree 'Crab' No 42727, heading a short freight, had just crossed the L&Y Liverpool - Preston line and was about to cross the CLC Southport Extension. Photograph J A Peden collection.

wheels and chains which provided the lift being housed in four stark sandstone towers. The plate girder bridge immediately on the landward side had the distinction of being the only structure which forced the Liverpool Overhead Railway down to street level for a short stretch.

A new coal depot near Blackstone Street opened in 1875 and a branch to additional coal drops in Bramley Moore Dock was brought into use during 1882, putting an extra burden on the single track. Doubling from Sandhills to Regent Road was thus unavoidable, and work was completed in April 1893. Horses worked the high level tracks until heavier rails were installed in 1895. Afterwards an L&Y pug pottering about or standing on Regent Road bridge became a familiar sight. North Docks goods depot acquired extensive cattle sidings which dealt with the bulk of Irish livestock landed at Liverpool.

Sometimes as many as 250 wagons a day were dispatched. However, following a serious outbreak of foot and mouth disease around the turn of the century, the government ordered that this traffic was to be transferred to Birkenhead where it could be quarantined.

The second dock branch was a piece of forward thinking by the L&Y; in fact it almost amounted to a gamble. An Act dated 17th May 1861 sanctioned a four and three quarter mile line from Fazakerley Junction on the Bury line to the shore just north of Bootle. At the time there were just sand dunes and fields here, and the nearest commercial activity was at Canada Dock well over a mile away. The Aintree & Bootle branch opened on 27th August 1866, intersecting the Preston and Southport lines on the way. A west to north spur from Sefton Junction to Aintree Station Junction provided

a connection with the former from the outset, whilst a flying east to south spur established a link with the latter between Marsh Lane and Seaforth stations during the 1880s.

From Fazakerley Junction double track headed west past Aintree racecourse then across Seeds Lane, climbing at 1 in 100 and partly on an embankment. The summit was at Warbreck Moor, close to the bridge over the Preston line. Beyond Sefton Junction the line fell at 1 in 150 and curved south westwards through a cutting bridged by Orrell Road. After passing beneath Hawthorne Road, the rails resumed an elevated course and spanned the Leeds & Liverpool canal, Linacre Road and the Southport line. Following a plate girder bridge over Crosby Road, the tracks veered southwards and a sandstone viaduct descended at 1 in 82 to street level. A large amount of land was acquired here for the fan of sidings which eventually developed.

Before long, Brocklebank, Langton, Alexandra and Hornby Docks had extended the port northwards to Bootle, and North Mersey & Alexandra Dock goods depot became very busy. A four storey warehouse was completed in 1884, an office building was erected in the south west corner near Strand Road, and a large granary was rail connected. Incoming cotton and machinery for dispatch were significant, but this was also the main yard in Liverpool for timber imports and in 1908 a huge electric cantilever crane was installed to deal with this traffic. It had a longitudinal run of 540 yards on 28 feet gauge track, and the 172 feet transverse span could lift and distribute up to 10 tons of timber. North Mersey was the haunt of two or three L&Y pugs which operated trip workings to and from Aintree yard.

Not content with capturing a large share of dock traffic north of Pier Head, the L&Y opened a substantial depot near Brunswick and Toxteth Docks during 1882. South Docks goods station stood at the corner of Sefton Street (the dock road) and Warwick Street, the LNWR and CLC Brunswick depots being close neighbours. It was served by two parallel tracks curving in from the MD&HB line and had the increasingly familiar iron framework clad with decorative brickwork.

The third and final branch to the northern group of docks was authorised in 1882, although its origins go back a further decade. In 1871 the L&Y established a depot at Bankfield to serve Canada Dock. Access was by way of MD&HB tracks along Regent Road, but the mandatory horse traction proved slow and inefficient. The mile long Bankfield branch from Bootle (later Oriel Road) station was part of a massive package of improvements which included quadrupling from Seaforth to Sandhills, the Seaforth spur, and Aintree and Fazakerley yards. Work began in spring 1884 and the

Part of the sprawling North Mersey goods yard on 3rd July 1958. Insulated meat containers on 'Conflats' in the left foreground, dereliction on the right, and ex-LMS 0-6-0Ts shunting the sidings in the distance.

The heavily embellished bridge carrying Fazakerley - North Mersey tracks across Warbreck Moor, the main road to Preston, in Aintree. This pre-World War 1 view is looking towards Liverpool. Racecourse station, off to the left, was only used once a year so it seems probable that the lettering 'Express service of trains to Manchester, Wigan, Bolton, Rochdale, Oldham, Halifax, Bradford, Leeds and all parts of Yorkshire' was taken down and stored after the Grand National. The preponderance of horse-drawn traffic explains the state of the road surface! Photograph J Ryan collection.

line was brought into use on 14th March 1887.

Establishing Bankfield & Canada Dock depot had meant demolishing the large and once isolated Stanley Hall, but several rows of terraced houses had to go for the branch itself. The line descended at 1 in 65 and 1 in 89, veering away from the Southport route to the south of Millers Bridge and curving steadily westwards at a low level through the grid of streets west of the main line. Three short 'cut and cover' tunnels were created at St John's Road (109 yards), Brasenose Road (67 yards) and Canal (51 yards), the last one predictably under the Leeds & Liverpool navigation. Intervening sections ran between massive retaining walls and the surviving houses in Ceres Street and Ivor Street were treated to the cacophony and copious exhaust of goods trains blasting out of Bankfield yard.

The last L&Y goods station built in Liverpool occupied a central position near the Custom House less than 500 yards from the LNWR Wapping complex. It was established principally to deal with full loads of cotton. In its final form, Wapping & Salthouse depot occupied a wedge of land between Canning Place, Mersey Street and the dock road, Ansdell Street bisecting the site. The southern section opened in 1901 and the remainder was completed during 1914. Shops and small industrial premises were cleared to make way for the depot. An ornate office building stood at the corner of Ansdell Street and a Y-shaped connection near Salthouse Lane led from MD&HB tracks. Traffic was worked to and from North Docks yard by L&Y pugs.

Returning to the 1870s and 1880s, the relentless increase in passenger and freight traffic, coupled with a desperate need to improve a woefully inadequate infrastructure, prompted the L&Y to embark on its massive investment programme. Quadrupling south of Walton Junction, the new Exchange station and other improvements already described, were manifestations of this bold scheme. The marshalling yard at Aintree, together with the sidings at Fazakerley and Sandhills, were also part of this grand plan. Aintree gridiron, comprising some 18 miles of track received wagons from all parts of the L&Y system, including an endless procession of coal trains from Lancashire pits hauled by big 0-8-0s. Smaller engines shuttled backwards and forwards between Aintree and the various dockside terminals with lesser loads. Between them, the sidings at Fazakerley and Sandhills alone could cope with over 3,000 wagons at a time.

Concentration of freight traffic at Aintree required a new engine shed near the yard. Eleven acres of land between the North Mersey branch and the spur to Aintree station was purchased from the CLC and the depot opened in 1886. It had eight roads under cover, a turntable, and five loco sidings. This supplemented Sandhills shed (more widely known as Bank Hall from 1920) which dated from around 1850 and was substantially rebuilt in 1873-74. Both the L&Y and East Lancashire provided small depots near Great Howard Street when their lines opened, but these only lasted until about 1876.

Much of the North Mersey branch was incorporated in the L&Y suburban electrification programme, the spur from Bootle and the Sefton Junction - Aintree chord also being energised. Local services between Exchange and Aintree commenced on 1st June 1906, six months before electric trains on the direct line via Walton Junction. New stations were provided at Linacre Road and Ford. The former served an area of Victorian terraces, whilst the latter stood at the west-

ern end of Aintree yard. Both were fairly basic affairs with timber platforms and tiny wooden shelters.

Passenger trains had in fact appeared on the North Mersey branch some years earlier. In 1890 an excursion station was built near Warbreck Moor for Grand National traffic. Aptly called Racecourse, it had a peculiar - maybe unique - arrangement. A long cinder platform was constructed alongside the inner edge of the line from Fazakerley Junction, and the slightly elevated eastbound track actually ran along the middle of it. Expenditure on this awkward embankment site was thus kept to a minimum and special arrangements involving one line working were brought into operation for the annual extravaganza. Finally, the North Mersey branch was electrified as far as a halt serving newly opened Gladstone Dock. From 7th September 1914 the single timber platform attached to the northern side of the curving viaduct above Regent Road was served by seven or eight trains a day.

The massive L&Y investment designed to exploit dock traffic at Liverpool took place over a sixty year period and from 1914 to 1939 the infrastructure remained more or less intact. Over the next forty years it was steadily dismantled, mirroring the decline of the port, and today precious little remains.

Electric trains to Gladstone Dock ceased on 7th July 1924, less than ten years after they were introduced. Nearby Seaforth Sands station on the Liverpool Overhead Railway was just a few hundred yards away and was far more popular with travellers from the city centre. The first goods depot to close was South Dock which was completely burnt out after an air raid on 26th September 1940. It was on fire for a couple of days and smouldered for weeks. The site is now occupied by new houses. In 1946 the newer warehouse at Wapping became premises for a motor firm and six years later the Goliath crane at North Mersey was scrapped.

Exchange to Aintree electric services via the North Mersey branch were withdrawn on 2nd April 1951 and Ford and Linacre Road stations closed. The remaining part of Wapping depot was abandoned on 22nd June 1959 and all traces have been obliterated by the Merseyside Police HQ. Racecourse station closed on 31st March 1962. North Docks finished as a general goods depot on 30th June 1963, although private sidings survived for a while. It then became a road transport base.

Great Howard Street goods closed on 30th September 1963. During the Victorian era this huge depot had become a maze of rails akin to a plate of spaghetti. Sidings were on two levels and some of them wriggled beneath the viaduct spans. Wagon turntables, acute curves, hoists, an incline, and several street crossings com-

Immediately after setting off from Aintree Racecourse station, rebuilt Royal Scot 4-6-0 No 46146 THE RIFLE BRIGADE (1A Willesden), piloted by Standard 2MT 2-6-0 No 78061 (27D Wigan L&Y), draw the empty stock of a Grand National special from Euston forward to Aintree sidings on 25th March 1961. The train is crossing the L&Y line between Walton Junction and Maghull which is being used by class 5 4-6-0 No 45415 (24E Blackpool) on a Liverpool Exchange-Preston working. In a few yards the empty race train will cross over the CLC line to Aintree Central. Photograph P Fitton.

bined to create numerous operating headaches. On 4th January 1965 Bankfield depot and the branch from Bootle were consigned to history, the site of the yard now being occupied by a huge grain silo. Regent Road lift bridge, which had been fixed since 1940, was last used by coal bound for the MD&HB tipplers on 1st October 1966, although sand and gravel traffic over the Wellington Dock branch continued for another nine years. As steam traction was abandoned, Bank Hall shed (27A) closed on 22nd October 1966, followed by Aintree (27B) on 12th June 1967. Finally, North Mersey goods depot finished on 10th June 1968, although again private sidings survived for a while. Nevertheless, most of the former Aintree & Bootle branch lasted until February 1994, to provide access to Fazakerley Engineers yard from the Southport line. A few relics of the dock branches can still be glimpsed from Northern Line electrics.

BANK HALL (27A) SHED ALLOCATION JANUARY 1954
Ex-LMS 2P 4-4-0: 40581, 40584, 40588, 40684
Ex-LMS Compound 4P 4-4-0: 41193
Ex-LMS Stanier 5MT 4-6-0: 44688, 44689, 44690, 44691, 44692, 44767, 45068, 45216, 45227, 45228, 45229
Ex-LMS Stanier Jubilee 6P 4-6-0: 45698 MARS, 45717 DAUNTLESS, 45719 GLORIOUS
Ivatt 2MT 2-6-0: 46406, 46414, 46416, 46417, 46435, 46483
Ex-LMS Kitson 0F 0-4-0ST: 47001, 47002
Ex-L&Y Aspinall 0F 0-4-0ST: 51206, 51216, 51227, 51229, 51231, 51232, 51234, 51237, 51246, 51253
Ex-L&Y Aspinall 2F 0-6-0ST: 51307, 51371, 51375, 51396
Ex L&Y Aspinall 1F 0-6-0T: 51546
Total 42

AINTREE (27B) SHED ALLOCATION JANUARY 1954
Ex-LMS Compound 4P 4-4-0: 41102, 41186, 41187, 41188
Ex-LMS Ivatt 2MT 2-6-2T: 41283, 41284
Ex-LMS Hughes/Fowler 5MT 2-6-0: 42726, 42727, 42728, 42732
Ex-LMS Fowler 7F 0-8-0: 49503, 49505, 49515, 49545, 49547, 49552, 49554, 49566, 49582, 49586, 49620, 49637, 49638, 49640, 49659, 49664, 49672
Ex-L&Y Aspinall 2P 2-4-2T: 50648
Ex L&Y Aspinall 2F 0-6-0ST: 51343, 51413, 51460, 51462, 51530
Ex L&Y Aspinall 1F 0-6-0T: 51535, 51537, 51544
Ex-L&Y Aspinall 3F 0-6-0: 52135, 52136, 52171, 52258, 52278, 52299, 52311, 52378, 52379, 52381, 52412, 52416
Ex-MoS WD Austerity 8F 2-8-0: 90216, 90278, 90282, 90687
Total 52

DEPARTURES FROM LIVERPOOL EXCHANGE
Monday to Saturday, July 1960
SO - Saturdays Only
SX - Saturdays Excepted

Southport trains shown are Mondays/Tuesdays/Thursdays/Fridays. The Saturday and Wednesday timetables were different, but variations have been excluded for simplicity, although the two late night trains on Saturday have been included. Note the frequent simultaneous departures. The three simultaneous departures at 1.30pm are as shown in the timetable.

1.45am Preston (non-stop, with connections for Glasgow/Edinburgh)
5.25am Southport Chapel Street
5.30am Ormskirk
5.50am Rochdale
6.00am Blackpool Central
6.10am Southport Chapel Street
6.15am Ormskirk
6.30am Southport Chapel Street
6.35am Ormskirk
6.50am Southport Chapel Street
6.50am Ormskirk
6.55am Rochdale
7.00am Ormskirk
7.04am Southport Chapel Street
7.10am Southport Chapel Street
7.22am Aintree Sefton Arms
7.30am Southport Chapel Street
7.34am Ormskirk
7.44am Southport Chapel Street
7.50am Southport Chapel Street
7.54am Ormskirk
7.56am Manchester Victoria
8.00am Southport Chapel Street
8.10am Windermere
8.10am Southport Chapel Street
8.12am Ormskirk
8.18am Southport Chapel Street
8.30am Bradford Exchange/Leeds Central
8.30am Southport Chapel Street
8.36am Blackpool North/Fleetwood
8.38am Hall Road
8.40am Ormskirk
8.50am Southport Chapel Street
8.55am Ormskirk
9.00am Hall Road
9.05am Rochdale (Scarborough Londesborough Road SO)
9.10am Southport Chapel Street
9.13am Blackburn
9.15am (SO) Glasgow Central
9.24am Ormskirk
9.30am Southport Chapel Street
9.40am (SX) Bradford Exchange/Leeds Central
9.43am Glasgow Central/Edinburgh Princes Street
9.50am Southport Chapel Street
9.50am Preston (Blackpool Central SO)
10.00am Ormskirk
10.00am (SO) Newcastle
10.10am Southport Chapel Street
10.30am Newcastle
10.30am Southport Chapel Street
10.40am Ormskirk
10.50am Southport Chapel Street
11.05am Blackpool Central
11.10am Southport Chapel Street
11.15am (SO) Windermere
11.17am Ormskirk
11.30am Southport Chapel Street
11.30am Bradford Exchange/Leeds Central
11.40am (SX) Wigan Wallgate
11.45am (Ormskirk)
11.50am Southport Chapel Street
11.58am (SO) Ormskirk
12.03pm (SO) Wigan Wallgate
12.08pm Ormskirk
12.10pm Southport Chapel Street
12.13pm (SO) Aintree Sefton Arms
12.20pm Southport Chapel Street
12.20pm (SX) Blackpool Central
12.25pm Ormskirk
12.30pm Southport Chapel Street
12.30pm Bradford Exchange
12.38pm (SX) Maghull

Rebuilt Patriot 4-6-0 No 45530 SIR FRANK REE (1B Camden) has just been turned on the 'table at Aintree shed on 25th March 1961, having brought the 1Z63 Grand National special from Euston to Aintree Racecourse station. Standard 2MT 2-6-0 No 78063 in the background had piloted the train from Wigan North Western. Photograph P Fitton.

12.40pm Southport Chapel Street
12.42pm Rochdale
12.47pm (SO) Ormskirk
12.50pm Southport Chapel Street
1.00pm Ormskirk
1.00pm Southport Chapel Street
1.10pm (SO) Blackpool Central
1.10pm Southport Chapel Street
1.15pm Ormskirk
1.25pm Aintree Sefton Arms
1.30pm Southport Chapel Street
1.30pm Preston
1.30pm (SO) Bradford Exchange
1.36pm Ormskirk
1.42pm (SO) Wigan Wallgate
1.50pm Southport Chapel Street
1.58pm Ormskirk
2.10pm Southport Chapel Street
2.15pm Glasgow Central
2.30pm Southport Chapel Street
2.30pm Bradford Exchange/Leeds Central
2.36pm Ormskirk
2.50pm Southport Chapel Street
2.57pm Ormskirk
3.00pm Bolton Trinity Street
3.10pm Southport Chapel Street
3.23pm (SX) Preston
3.30pm Southport Chapel Street
3.30pm Bradford Exchange/Leeds Central
3.35pm Ormskirk
3.50pm Southport Chapel Street
3.50pm (SO) Ormskirk
4.00pm Southport Chapel Street
4.00pm Rochdale
4.03pm Preston
4.05pm (SX) Wigan Wallgate
4.10pm Southport Chapel Street
4.12pm Ormskirk
4.17pm Southport Chapel Street
4.30pm Bradford Exchange/Leeds Central
4.30pm Southport Chapel Street - limited stop
4.32pm Southport Chapel Street

4.35pm Glasgow Central/Edinburgh Princes Street
4.40pm Southport Chapel Street
4.40pm Blackpool Central/Skipton
4.45pm Ormskirk
4.50pm Southport Chapel Street
4.50pm (SX) Aintree Sefton Arms
4.53pm Bolton Trinity Street
4.59pm Hall Road
5.00pm (SX) Fleetwood/Windermere
5.02pm Southport Chapel Street - limited stop
5.02pm Ormskirk
5.05pm Southport Chapel Street
5.06pm (SX) Aintree Sefton Arms
5.10pm Southport Chapel Street
5.11pm Ormskirk
5.17pm Southport Chapel Street
5.19pm (SX) Ormskirk
5.21pm Hall Road
5.22pm (SX) Wigan Wallgate
5.28pm Southport Chapel Street
5.30pm Southport Chapel Street - limited stop
5.30pm Ormskirk
5.36pm Southport Chapel Street
5.36pm (SX) Aintree Sefton Arms
5.39pm Hall Road
5.40pm Rochdale
5.43pm Southport Chapel Street
5.45pm Workington Main
5.48pm (SX) Ormskirk
5.50pm Southport Chapel Street
5.55pm Ormskirk
5.56pm Southport Chapel Street
6.02pm Southport Chapel Street
6.05pm (SX) Ormskirk
6.05pm (SX) Wigan Wallgate
6.10pm Southport Chapel Street
6.15pm Ormskirk
6.20pm Southport Chapel Street
6.28pm (SX) Aintree Sefton Arms
6.30pm Southport Chapel Street

6.30pm York
6.40pm Southport Chapel Street
6.40pm Ormskirk
6.48pm (SO) Manchester Victoria
6.50pm Southport Chapel Street
6.56pm (SX) Manchester Victoria
7.10pm Southport Chapel Street
7.15pm Ormskirk
7.25pm (SX) Ormskirk
7.30pm Southport Chapel Street
7.40pm Preston
7.50pm Southport Chapel Street
7.50pm (SO) Bolton Trinity Street
7.55pm Ormskirk
8.02pm (SX) Manchester Victoria
8.10pm Southport Chapel Street
8.20pm Ormskirk
8.20pm (SO) Manchester Victoria
8.30pm Southport Chapel Street
8.50pm Ormskirk
8.50pm Southport Chapel Street
9.05pm (SX) Blackpool Central
9.10pm Southport Chapel Street
9.10pm (SO) Blackpool Central
9.12pm Manchester Victoria
9.20pm Ormskirk
9.30pm Southport Chapel Street
9.40pm (SO) Ormskirk
9.50pm Southport Chapel Street
10.00pm Ormskirk
10.10pm Southport Chapel Street
10.15pm (SO) Rochdale
10.25pm Ormskirk
10.30pm Southport Chapel Street
10.50pm Southport Chapel Street
10.55pm Ormskirk
11.10pm Southport Chapel Street
11.25pm Ormskirk
11.30pm Southport Chapel Street
11.40pm (SO) Southport Chapel Street
11.55pm (SO) Southport Chapel Street

Cheshire Lines System in Liverpool

© Paul Anderson 1996

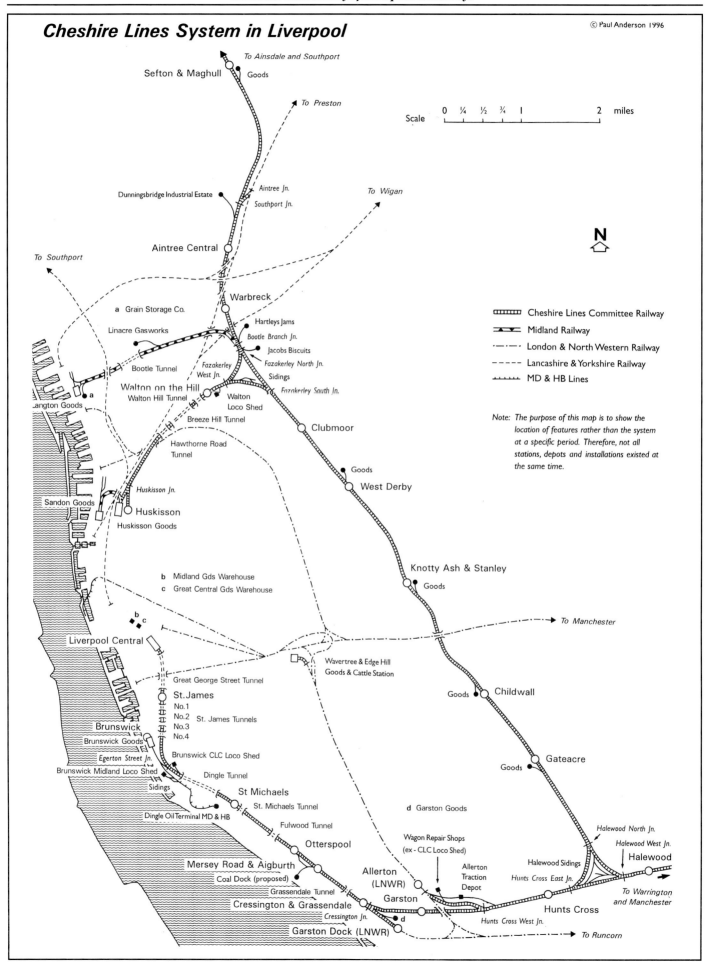

To Ainsdale and Southport

Sefton & Maghull   Goods

To Preston

Scale 0 ¼ ½ ¾ 1   2 miles

Dunningsbridge Industrial Estate

Aintree Jn.
Southport Jn.

To Southport

Aintree Central

To Wigan

Warbreck

a Grain Storage Co.

Hartleys Jams
Bootle Branch Jn.

Linacre Gasworks

Jacobs Biscuits
Fazakerley North Jn.

Fazakerley
West Jn.

Bootle Tunnel

Sidings

Walton on the Hill   Fazakerley South Jn.

Walton Hill Tunnel   Walton
Loco Shed

...angton Goods   a

Breeze Hill Tunnel

Clubmoor

Hawthorne Road
Tunnel

Goods

Huskisson Jn.

West Derby

Sandon Goods

Huskisson

Huskisson Goods

b Midland Gds Warehouse
c Great Central Gds Warehouse

Knotty Ash & Stanley

Goods

b c

To Manchester

Liverpool Central

Wavertree & Edge Hill
Goods & Cattle Station

Great George Street Tunnel

Childwall

St. James   Goods

No.1
No.2   St. James Tunnels
No.3
No.4

Brunswick

Brunswick Goods

Gateacre

Goods

Brunswick CLC Loco Shed

Egerton Street Jn.

Brunswick Midland Loco Shed

Dingle Tunnel

Sidings

St Michaels

Dingle Oil Terminal MD & HB

St. Michaels Tunnel

d Garston Goods

Fulwood Tunnel

Wagon Repair Shops
(ex - CLC Loco Shed)

Halewood North Jn.
Halewood West Jn.

Otterspool

Allerton
Traction
Depot

Halewood Sidings

Halewood

Mersey Road & Aigburth

Allerton
(LNWR)

Hunts Cross East Jn.

To Warrington
and Manchester

Coal Dock (proposed)

Garston

Grassendale Tunnel

Cressington & Grassendale

Hunts Cross

Cressington Jn.   d   Hunts Cross West Jn.

Garston Dock (LNWR)   To Runcorn

Key

▥▥▥▥	Cheshire Lines Committee Railway
▲▼▲	Midland Railway
─·─·─	London & North Western Railway
─ ─ ─	Lancashire & Yorkshire Railway
┼┼┼┼	MD & HB Lines

Note: The purpose of this map is to show the location of features rather than the system at a specific period. Therefore, not all stations, depots and installations existed at the same time.

N

Chapter 3
CHESHIRE LINES

The frontage of Liverpool Central in Ranelagh Street on 15th August 1969, with the former Mersey Railway Central Low Level station entrance to the right. Liverpool Corporation Leyland L231 en route from Kirkby to Pier Head passes the parcels office, whilst the bulk of Lewis' department store looms in the background. Posters advertised trains to Blackpool and North Wales for those contemplating a late summer holiday. Photograph J A Sommerfield.

The third main line system serving Liverpool was that operated by the Cheshire Lines Committee. This originated as a consortium of the Manchester, Sheffield & Lincolnshire (later Great Central) Railway and Great Northern Railway in 1863 and was formed three years later when the Midland Railway joined. It opened in stages between 1864 and 1884, duplicating the LNWR network in many respects, but also thrusting feelers into L&Y territory. Like its rivals, the CLC started off with an inconvenient passenger terminus (in this case Brunswick at the end of a branch from Garston) which was soon replaced by much larger facilities in the city centre. Again like the LNWR and L&Y, the newcomer also had a main line to Manchester which carried through services for Yorkshire and other parts of England. Goods depots were established in both the southern and northern docks, access to the latter being by way of a line skirting Liverpool, roughly parallel to the LNWR Bootle branch but a mile or so further east. Finally, an attempt was made to compete with the L&Y for Southport traffic, but the route proved an indirect one to say the least. It did however pass through Aintree and saw plenty of passengers on Grand National days.

It has often been the case of last in, first out, as far as railways are concerned and, indeed, much of the former CLC system in Merseyside has been dismantled, including the passenger terminus at Liverpool Central. For several years the erstwhile main line approach through Garston and St Michaels also lay derelict, but it was eventually rescued and incorporated in the Merseyrail electric network. East of Garston the CLC route remained busy, trains from Lime Street to Manchester Piccadilly and beyond using the spur at Allerton. It now carries the principal passenger services between Liverpool and Manchester.

GARSTON & LIVERPOOL
The CLC story begins with that unassuming company, the St Helens Canal & Railway, which featured in Chapter 1. It will be recalled that interest in the local line as a potentially strategic route was widespread, especially after the extensions to Garston and Manchester were completed in 1854-56. The Manchester Sheffield & Lincolnshire Railway soon began running local trains to Garston over the St Helens tracks and during 1858 a service from London Kings Cross was put on by the Great Northern. This was met by an 'express omnibus' which conveyed passengers to North John Street in Liverpool city

Mersey Road & Aigburth station, looking towards Liverpool in the early 1900s. The original Garston & Liverpool building stands high above the cutting. Advertisements for cocoa, easy chairs, Player's cigarettes, matches, pianos and soap decorate the retaining wall. Photograph J F Ward collection.

The magnificent CLC Brunswick goods station at the corner of Sefton Street and Northumberland Street embraced the original Garston & Liverpool passenger terminus, still bearing the legend BRUNSWICK STATION CHESHIRE LINES RAILWAY. With a ground floor area of almost 160,000 square feet, the depot was over one hundred and fifteen times the size of the older building. The lettering along the frontage read 'GREAT NORTHERN, MANCHESTER SHEFFIELD & LINCOLNSHIRE & MIDLAND RAILWAYS'. South Docks L&Y goods, destroyed in the war, was away to the left beyond the pub. This view, looking south, was taken on 15th August 1971. Photograph J F Ward.

centre and in 1858/59 the MS&L provided a ferry from Garston to The Pier Head.

With long distance travellers on competing routes leaving their trains at Lime Street or Exchange, the inconvenient transfers at Garston were clearly unsatisfactory. From September 1859, GN through coaches and goods wagons were worked over the LNWR's Liverpool & Manchester line. Furthermore, both the GN and MS&L opened offices at various stations, including Lime Street, Wapping and Waterloo. Despite this foothold in the centre of Liverpool, the use of 'foreign' mileage and depots was an unattractive proposition when viewed long term, so a meeting was convened during March 1861 to muster support for a new railway north of Garston. The Garston & Liverpool Railway duly received its Act of Parliament on 17th May 1861. It was to be a four mile double track line with a terminus at Queen's Dock, although this was altered to Brunswick Dock in 1862.

In its own way, the Garston & Liverpool was a remarkable length of railway. With a journey no more than half a mile from the Mersey shore, passengers might have expected fine views over the estuary towards the Wirral from their carriage window, but virtually the whole line was in a shallow rock cutting punctuated by tunnels. It also crept unobtrusively through the former Cressington and Dingle estates where, even in the early 1920s, there were *'quiet roads down which it was a soothing pleasure on a summer's evening to wind along between their mossy red sandstone walls with a line of grand old trees arching overhead, past grassy demesne and wooded estate, past snug cottage house, dairy and poultry farm'* according to one writer. There was also the 'latticed and stuccoed oasis' of St Michael's Hamlet, the wooded dell at Otterspool and the sandy cove at Knotts Hole. This was hardly a typical railway approach to a busy port!

Considering the amount of excavation required, construction proceeded fairly rapidly and the line was ready at the end of 1863. However, there was some delay in agreeing junction arrangements with the St Helens Railway (which had been leased by the LNWR since 1860) so the Garston & Liverpool finally opened without ceremony on 1st June 1864. Free horse buses conveyed passengers and luggage from Brunswick to Lower Castle Street where the company had its offices. Shortly afterwards, the newly formed CLC established its headquarters at James Street and provided a booking office and waiting room for passengers on the Garston line.

From an end-on junction with a spur off the St Helens line, the Brunswick route headed north westwards and immediately entered the long cutting which would take it all the way to Dingle. A high stone bridge over Otterspool dell was followed by Fulwood Tunnel (200 yards) which hid the railway from the secluded villas of Fulwood Park. St Michaels Tunnel (103 yards) did the same for St Michael's Hamlet. Dingle Tunnel (1,082 yards) led the line through a spur of sandstone down to the shore and docks. Several elegant sandstone and brick arches with an almost oval profile carried lanes leading to cottages by the beach. There were no sharp curves and the steepest gradient was 1 in 200.

Three intermediate stations were provided in 1864 - Mersey Road (Mersey Road & Aigburth from 1880), Otter's Pool (Otterspool from 1866) and St Michaels. The last named was on an overbridge across the tracks, whilst the other two stood on the eastern side of the cutting. All were in red brick and featured round-headed windows, steeply pitched slate roofs and tall chimneys, the decorative bargeboards and general plan revealing MS&L influence. Brick walls lined the cutting at the back of the platforms. Brunswick terminus on Sefton Street was totally different. It consisted of a rather austere three storey block with pronounced quoins (corner stones) and rectangular windows set off by prominent and quite decorative casements. Triangular pediments finished off the gable ends and similar but smaller features surmounted doorways.

Another intermediate station opened at Cressington on 1st March 1873 and it was a gem of suburban railway architecture. The building stood in the Cressington Park estate and was approached by a driveway past a private entrance lodge. Grassendale estate stretched away towards the Mersey beyond the railway and was acknowledged when the station name was changed to Cressington & Grassendale in 1877. Such refined surroundings demanded something special and the architect clearly rose to the challenge. The compact main building was impressive enough at street level, but it formed a tower when seen from the platforms. Half-hipped steeply-pitched roofs gave the structure its overall character - that of a rather bulky cottage - but exquisite details added a special air, in keeping with the nearby estates. There was some very detailed fretwork along the eaves, the windows and doorways had pointed gothic arches and the tall chimneys seemed to swell from the roofs.

Even before the line from Garston opened, it was obvious that Brunswick would not be able to match Lime Street and Exchange as a terminus for main line passengers. Therefore, parliamentary approval was sought for a difficult and costly extension to the middle of the city. The Liverpool Central Station & Railway was authorised in 1864 and is described in the next part of this chapter. Meanwhile the Garston & Liverpool purchased the Wavertree estate near Edge Hill in order to build a cattle station, approached by a short branch off the LNWR's newly opened Edge Hill-Speke line, over which running powers were granted. GN/MS&L running powers from Timperley to Garston over the LNWR were also stipulated in the original Garston & Liverpool Act, thus guaranteeing the partners a through Manchester-Liverpool route. Access to Lime Street, Waterloo and Wapping continued as well.

These various running powers and the impending extension to Liverpool Central began to irritate the LNWR and the company became awkward. In October 1864 it locked the GN/MS&L offices at Waterloo, thus preventing the clerks from carrying out their duties. Then the Wapping office was closed and papers left scattered on the floor. In January 1865 the allies were told to withdraw staff from Lime Street and send traffic only via Warrington. Two passenger trains continued to use Lime Street, but the LNWR did not show them in the timetable, refused to service the coaches, and would not allow local Liverpool-Manchester passengers to board them. They continued, on MS&L insistence, but made a heavy loss and were withdrawn in October 1865, much to the relief of the GN.

Independent access to Liverpool was becoming of paramount importance and the first stage came on 5th July 1865 with the Cheshire Lines Transfer Act. The Garston & Liverpool Railway and Liverpool Central Station & Railway were vested jointly with the GN and MS&L, together with four local lines in Cheshire (Cheshire Midland, West Cheshire, Stockport & Woodley Junction and Stockport, Timperley & Altrincham Junction). On 6th July 1865 the MS&L (Extension to Liverpool) Act was passed, thus sanctioning the much needed independent main line from Manchester to Liverpool. Finally, on 18th July 1866, the Cheshire Lines Committee was authorised. This took over the MS&L extension to Liverpool as well as the joint GN/MS&L lines and admitted the Midland Railway as a formidable third partner.

Considering the overwhelming need for the CLC main line, it got off to a very hesitant start - partly because capital was scarce during the recession precipitated by the American Civil War. MS&L enthusiasm was waning and in 1868 the company proposed a deal with the LNWR over access to Lime Street, Edge Hill and the docks. But the GN and Midland dismissed this idea and construction work began. The line ran for just over 28 miles, from Cornbrook Junction on the Manchester-Altrincham branch, to Cressington Junction on the former Garston & Liverpool. It included three viaducts and two tunnels, but the steepest gradient was a modest 1 in 132.

By mid-1871 most of the earthworks had been completed, although a shortage of labour and prolonged heavy rain at the end of 1872 hampered progress. Goods traffic began on 1st March 1873 and passenger services between Liverpool Brunswick and Manchester London Road began on 1st August 1873. A half mile spur to the LNWR at Allerton opened on 14th May 1873, providing easier access to the CLC cattle station at Wavertree Road. This depot was expanded to cater for general goods traffic in 1876 and was renamed Wavertree & Edge Hill on 1st January 1890.

In the Liverpool area, three passenger stations were provided during 1874 and two of them were quite remarkable. Garston opened at the beginning of April, incorporating a fascinating brick and stone entrance block on Woolton Road; it featured three steeply pitched roofs, two of them parallel and the other at right angles, all of them capped with ornate iron cresting. With the exception of one of the ends, they were finished off with stepped

Herculaneum Dock, looking south east from the iron bridge that spanned Brunswick shed yard, on 15th August 1971. Dingle oil storage tanks are prominent in the distance, the track serving them running at the foot of the retaining wall. Dingle CLC tunnel is off to the left, whilst the cavity to the left of the dock gates marked the entrance to the Liverpool Overhead Dingle tunnel, its lattice bridge approach having long been demolished. Photograph J F Ward.

Ex-Great Central class D11 'Large Director' 4-4-0 No 62662 PRINCE OF WALES on arrival at Liverpool Central with a stopping train from Stockport Tiviot Dale, 4th April 1953. The airy roof span and Newington bridge complete the scene. Photograph S Creer.

Smartly turned out ex-LMS 4F 0-6-0 No 44407 of Heaton Mersey shed at Liverpool Central with a local from Warrington Central, 31st March 1956. A Stanier 3MT 2-6-2T has coupled on to the rear of the train, ready to take out the empty stock. Photograph S Creer.

The exit from Liverpool Central in terminal decline on 20th August 1971. Track has already been removed from platforms 1 and 2, and only one set of polished metals enters Great George Street tunnel. Incredibly, the soot caked ramshackle buildings overlooking the station signal cabin had smart facades on fashionable Bold Street. Photograph J A Sommerfield.

gables, each of the steps having its own little 'roof' creating a serrated effect from a distance. A bulbous stone finial rose from each apex and thistle-like iron finials surmounted these. The remaining gable, over the entrance, had three sloping triangular faces. The entrance porch was a smaller yet even more ornate version of the stepped gables. Windows were a mixture of rectangular Tudor and pointed gothic styles. A parapet masked the eaves and one of the chimney stacks was in the form of an inverted Y, akin to flying buttresses. Inside, the building was just as elaborate. Four flights of iron-banistered stairs descended to platform level around a white-tiled well below an open-raftered roof with a central hanging finial.

Hunts Cross, opened in May 1874, was less ornate but just as interesting. The two storey red brick facade on Speke Road had a fairly bland appearance, relieved by peaked dormer windows. However, the railway was in a substantial cutting here and the rear elevation rose to a towering four storeys. An unusual decorative iron balcony was provided at first floor level and stairs led down to the platform. In 1881 additional goods lines were laid between Hunts Cross West Junction (where the Allerton spur went off) and Halewood, thus quadrupling this section of the main line. As a result Hunts Cross station was provided with extra platforms and Halewood, also opened in May 1874, was rebuilt.

Initially the CLC hired carriages and wagons from the owning partners, but soon purchased its own rolling stock. By the grouping of 1923 it had nearly 600 coaches and over 4,000 goods vehicles on its books. Many of the former were used on Liverpool-Manchester expresses and they exuded luxury. Handsome composites built by the Lancaster Carriage & Wagon Company had first class compartments lined in mahogany and upholstered with green or brown velvet, whilst the exceptionally fine coaches supplied by Great Central workshops (in 1914) featured first class accommodation finished in walnut and sycamore with fittings of oxidised copper and deep blue cloth seats. Such opulence was understandable in view of the popularity of the CLC service, but this was only possible because of the extension to Liverpool Central.

CENTRAL

The Liverpool Central Station & Railway received its Act on 29th July 1864, but passengers had to endure the inconvenient and often annoying horse bus transfer from Brunswick to James Street for another decade. For six years no construction work took place, although this is understandable in view of the time-consuming detailed planning and land purchases that were necessary. The line was barely a mile and a half long, but the bulk of it was in a series of tunnels through red

ANGLICAN CATHEDRAL

The rear of Brunswick shed on 27th February 1955, showing O4/8 2-8-0 No 63721 and O4/3 2-8-0 No 63739. The constricted site meant that the depot was built on a curve and another unusual feature was the provision of five roads under cover (odd numbers, except three, were rarely found in British practice). Photograph F W Shuttleworth.

sandstone and most of the remainder ran through cuttings 38 to 48 feet deep. Furthermore, Liverpool Corporation had managed to get a clause inserted in the Act prohibiting the use of explosives for excavation purposes.

The contract was awarded in July 1870 and the daunting task began almost immediately. From Egerton Street Junction, about a third of a mile short of Brunswick terminus, the line curved northwards and passed under Caryl Street at an acute angle. The track was already in a steep-sided cutting which was spanned by a bridge carrying Park Street. St James No 4 Tunnel (211 yards) took the line below Grafton Street and Northumberland Street and it emerged in a 15 yard sheerwalled gap which replaced eleven houses on Star Street and Upper Mann Street.

St James No 3 Tunnel (153 yards) and St James No 2 Tunnel (172 yards) were bored beneath Warwick Street and Beaufort Street respectively. They were separated by another sandstone chasm, this time of 32 yards, where seventeen houses on Chapman Street and Beaufort Street once stood. Beyond St James No 2 a 50 yard gap requiring the demolition of fourteen back-to-backs off Brassey Street and a couple of dwellings on Hill Street led to St James No 1 Tunnel (185 yards). The next break (97 yards) stretched from Stanhope Street to Parliament Street and was somewhat wider as it accommodated the platforms of St James station. Just to complicate matters, Ashwell Street was carried across the cutting by a sandstone arch.

Finally, at 1,320 yards, came Great George Street Tunnel, the longest on the Cheshire Lines system. Most of it was excavated below the full length of Great George Street, although the sharply curved northern end passed beneath Seel Street, Fleet Street and Bold Street at an angle. The tracks emerged obliquely near Roscoe Place. Near Duke Street the CLC tunnel encountered the LNWR Wapping branch, also in a tunnel and at a slightly lower level, necessitating a subterranean bridge. Three tracks were provided on the extension from Garston, one for incoming trains, one for departures, and a middle line for light engine and empty stock movements. With rising gradients as steep as 1 in 90, the approach to Central

The highly ornate and rather strange exterior of Garston CLC station, 21st April 1950. Photograph H C Casserley.

The main line platforms at Hunts Cross, looking towards Liverpool on 22nd July 1957. Just visible on the left is the remarkably tall main building, while a fine example of Macfarlane's patent cast iron 'Gents' in the 'decorated' style is prominent on the island platform. Electric trains from Southport Chapel Street now terminate on the far side of the island platform where services from Southport Lord Street, Aintree and Gateacre once called. Photograph J A Peden.

Ex-LNER J39 0-6-0 No 64748 of Gorton, provided with a Great Central tender, passes Gateacre with a train of hoppers bound for Clarence Dock Power Station on 29th March 1958. The station was unique on the North Liverpool line in having its platforms connected by a subway. A covered walkway linked the down platform to the main building, the intervening space being reserved for quadrupling that never came. Photograph J A Peden.

could become foul in certain conditions. The site of the terminus was a wedge-shaped area between Ranelagh Street, Renshaw Street and Bold Street. It consisted of 5.5 acres of prime commercial land in the heart of the city (Central was a very apt suffix) and negotiations for property purchase were not concluded until the end of 1869. Numerous buildings such as Waterloo Hotel and Roscoe Arcade had to be demolished, but the Lyceum and businesses on the east side of Bold Street were saved. In common with the approach line, a lot of rock had to be removed to accommodate the station and a maze of sewers, water mains and gas pipes needed diverting. Sandstone from the excavation was used to build the station walls.

It was quite an achievement to fit the platform accommodation and passenger facilities required at Central into the space available. The actual area occupied by the station was hemmed in by Cropper Street (parallel to Renshaw Street) and an alley known as Back Bold Street. These almost converged, thus creating a triangular site varying from a reasonable 90 yards at the inner end to a tight 38 yards at the throat, with just 250 yards separating the concourse from the tunnel mouth. By way of contrast, Lime Street station in its final form was 140 yards wide and Exchange station stretched for some 500 yards from the booking hall to the approach viaduct. A thoroughfare known as Newington crossed the station midway by a plate girder footbridge.

Despite these limitations, room was found for three island platforms at Central. Nos 1 and 2 on the west side were the longest and primarily dealt with main line arrivals. They incorporated a roadway for cabs and mail vans. Nos 3 and 4 were the principal departure platforms, whilst local services largely used Nos 5 and 6. A dock for horses, milk and similar traffic occupied the extreme north east corner.

Most of the station was covered by a handsome arched roof with a 164 feet span and a maximum height of 65 feet. This consisted of curved lattice ribs tied by arc shaped rods and radial struts which were reflected in the end screen. On the western side it sprang from the sandstone wall below Back Bold Street and in the east was supported by decorative iron columns between platforms 5 and 6. A lesser roof covered the remaining wedge near Cropper Street. With a generous amount of glazing, the station was light and airy when the panes were kept clean.

The interior of Central presented a very different appearance to the frontage on Ranelagh Street. This consisted of a three storey block set at an angle to the roadway, and the architecture was sombre rather than light-hearted. Heavy stonework and repetitive round-headed or rectangular windows dominated the facade, although a modicum of relief was provided by pilasters (attached columns) which divided the building into seven bays. The only concentrated ornamentation was along the roofline, where a delicate balustrade was enhanced by urn finials and a very distinctive Baroque clock surround. Two detached buildings, also in a severe classical style, stood in the fore-

court and accommodated the parcels office and refreshment rooms respectively. The CLC had its head office in the upper storeys of the main structure.

Liverpool Central opened on 1st March 1874, although only platforms 1 and 2 were ready, the remainder coming into use on 25th June. St James station, briefly mentioned earlier, opened at the same time as the terminus. Its platforms were in a grim cavern between two of the tunnels, but above was a still fashionable residential area of the city and the sandstone building at street level was in a sympathetic Georgian style, featuring a fine arcaded entrance.

Initially there were sixteen trains each way between Central and Manchester London Road, but services increased steadily over the next three decades and by 1907 the terminus was dealing with about 85 departures and the same number of arrivals every weekday. Compared with Lime Street and Exchange this was a fairly modest total and a solitary signal cabin with less than ninety levers sufficed. Unlike those of the rival LNWR and L&Y systems, the CLC approach to Liverpool remained fairly straightforward and had few feeder lines. However, at busy times the number of light engine movements began to cause problems and before long enough ground was found for a turntable and extra loco sidings in a corner near the tunnel mouth.

During its first two decades the extension experienced several developments, some minor, some significant and others unrealised. In 1882 parts of the retaining walls at Central were found to be in danger of collapse and piers supporting the roof were replaced by concrete. Walls at Brunswick were heightened about the same time to stop stone throwing. Brunswick passenger station closed on 1st March 1874 and became part of the goods depot. Around the turn of the century the building was incorporated in a colossal CLC goods depot, one of the largest structures in Liverpool. A connection to the dock lines was put in during 1884, access to Herculaneum Dock being especially important because of the vast amount of coal traffic - much of it for bunkering ships. The LUSITANIA and MAURETANIA, for example, burned about a thousand tons of fuel a day and required 6,000 tons for a trans-Atlantic crossing.

Then came a couple of interesting but potentially expensive proposals to link the extension with other lines. The first plan, devised by the MS&L in 1884, was to construct a line from St Michaels to the infant Mersey Railway (see Chapter 4), thus giving the CLC access to Birkenhead. Both the GN and Midland were interested at first, but when the project was expanded during 1887 to include an underground line to Huskisson the Kings Cross and Derby boards cooled. Had this latter line been built, the CLC would have been able to operate a circular suburban service via the North Liverpool tracks (see later) and cut some twelve miles off the journey to Southport. One development that did come about was the extension of the Mersey Railway to an underground terminus below platforms 1 and 2 at Liverpool Central, with a direct flight of stairs from the main line station. This was originally known as Liverpool Central Low Level, and remains an important interchange point on the Merseyrail network.

Edwardian years saw train services over the CLC at their peak. Although certainly not the busiest Liverpool terminus, Central was the most colourful, and maybe the most romantic. Pride of place went to the hourly service to Manchester which had been inaugurated on 9th July 1877. With 34 miles of largely straight and level track - and few junctions - it became a model of inter-urban running. In 1907 there were twenty trains each way, most of them taking 45 minutes (with a stop at Warrington). The odd ones avoiding Warrington did the journey in 40 minutes, thus matching LNWR and L&Y timings between the two cities. MS&L Sacre single-wheelers with lightweight coaches built up an enviable reputation for punctuality which the CLC stressed in advertisements, but as the heavier coaches described earlier came into use, GC 4-4-0s were introduced to maintain schedules.

In 1907 each of the partners ran trains to London. The GN contribution was largely symbolic, with the one Kings Cross working taking over six hours. The GC also operated a solitary service to Marylebone, with two in the opposite direction. However, the Midland expresses to St Pancras were much acclaimed and although the 4 hours 20 minutes timing was considerably slower than the non-stop runs from Lime Street, passengers were conveyed in unabashed luxury.

Local services ran to Warrington and Walton on the Hill, and there were the roundabout workings to Southport via Hunts Cross and Gateacre. These could hardly compete with the L&Y electrics for through passengers, but numerous intermediate stations generated plenty of short distance journeys. Midland and GC semi-fasts went to Sheffield via Chinley and Woodhead respectively. Special excursions - both incoming from Lancashire and Cheshire towns and outwards to Southport - were also handled, especially at Bank Holidays. In August 1907 there were 43 in one day, dead mileage being minimised by the empty stock of one train arriving behind the loco of the next.

Cross-country trains were also a familiar sight at Central in 1907. The GC ran through services to Norwich, Yarmouth, Lowestoft, Cromer and Harwich via Lincoln, Spalding and the Great Eastern Railway, some of them luncheon car expresses. A Midland train also ran to Cromer via Melton Mowbray, Bourne and the Midland & Great Northern Joint line. Even more significant were the workings from Hull and Grimsby, the former often arriving at Liverpool behind North Eastern Railway locos. From the early 1890s they brought waves of eastern European migrants crossing England on the way to America, and the scene at the Merseyside stage of their journey was vividly brought to life by John Pendleton in his 1896 book *Our Railways*:

Railway travel develops many interesting situations; but it has created few more bewildering than those occasionally to be seen during the Russian famine, when a number of peasantry, weary of the Czar's despotic rule and black bread, or no bread at all, came through England on their way to America, and clustered, apparently hopeless, on the platform at the Central station. They were in costumes that, in spite of their crumpled shabbiness, recalled the garb of Count Arnheim in the opera of 'The Bohemian Girl', and looked like fugitive kings and emperors beside the thick-set railway porter, in capacious velveteens, whose duty it was to put them on the right track towards the 'free land'. What the Russians thought of their rough but kindly guide it is impossible to say; but he grinned, and exclaimed in amazement as he tried in vain, with a stumpy pencil to get a list of their names, and then sympathetically remarked, as he looked at their wan faces, 'There is no wonder at the chaps being ill; even their names is all coughs and sneezes'. The CLC carried numerous passengers heading for steamer services from Liverpool, notably those to the Isle of Man and Llandudno in summer and Dublin and Belfast overnight all year. Furthermore, there were plenty of business travellers destined for trans-Atlantic liners in addition to the emigrants. Boat trains to Central were hardly worthy of the title because of the road transfer, but at least the CLC explored a couple of options for reaching the quays. On 20th January 1895 a nine coach special made up of three vehicles from each of the partners ventured along the MD&HB line from Brunswick to Riverside to see if through workings were feasible. Apparently the train was regarded as a traction engine by the dock authority and proceeded at 4mph behind a man with a red flag. The high officials on board suffered considerable indignity and the experiment was abandoned. Through coaches to Pier Head station on the Liverpool Overhead Railway via a connection at Brunswick was possible in theory, but the elevated structure was not designed to take 25 ton main line coaches. Instead, well-appointed wagonettes continued to convey passengers to the boats and there were few complaints.

There was a serious accident on the subterranean approach to Central during 1913. On 15th October a Cheshire Lines train was stationary at St James when the following Midland express to St Pancras ploughed into the rear of it, killing six passengers. On a lighter note, a CLC sign at the terminus could have been taken as an insult by certain people: *These closets are intended for the convenience of passengers only. Workmen, cabmen, fishporters and idlers are not permitted to use them.*

Between 1909 and 1913 a lengthy loop was installed between Mersey Road and Otterspool stations, together with a siding to serve a large new coaling dock then under construction. After a considerable amount of work had been done, the firm went into liquidation in 1913 and the project was abandoned. This would no doubt have brought a great deal of extra traffic to the CLC.

With the grouping of 1923, the CLC came under joint LMS/LNER control, but competition for Liverpool-Manchester traffic remained just as strong despite the fact that the former LNWR and L&Y routes were now in the hands of the LMS. Pre-grouping company loyalties persisted, and there is a hint of this in the wartime recollections which follow, those of a driver at Brunswick shed:

The Second World War dealt harshly with Liverpool. The docks and the houses gathered about endured bombing as terrible as any experienced in Britain and the dock workers at Brunswick were driven to find refuge in the nearby tunnels, much as their contemporaries in London's East End huddled together in the Tube. Two 4.5 inch anti-aircraft guns, set up at the nearby Herculaneum dock, crashed out nightly, adding to the general tumult; it was frequently terrifying to be around the shed at night but trips to Southport (on the CLC) could prove a respite, at least for the LNER men. Lunch on the bowling green was an unreal experience, as smoke drifted across the ruins of Liverpool. The Luftwaffe, it was clear, would never dare assault Southport. A tank engine on these runs made for light work but steam railcars, without names and in CLC colours, would often be turned out, with an extra coach. This usually ruined the bowling green lunch, such was the attention necessary to the unit, whilst the extra exertion demanded of the machine could bring flames leaping to the very mouth of the chimney. At night this was brought immediately to the attention of the ARP man and baffles were fitted, which served principally to reduce already unpromising steaming to wholly ineffective levels.

Liverpool was the principal point of ingress for many of the convoys hurrying across the Atlantic, fighting men in especial, and Brunswick crews, both LMS and LNER, took a considerable part in the work. American troops, mouths gaping at the destruction about them, were hauled off by V2 2-6-2s manned by Brunswick drivers and firemen.

The workings at Brunswick were thoroughly distorted by War but the strict divisions of the pre-war years between the LMS and LNER were not greatly broken down. The men remained attached to traditionally separate routes, which inhibited 'integration' but repairs and examinations and the division of space between the two concerns could be ordered with greater facility. The old Midland shed stood nearby and had been largely abandoned but it repeatedly proved of use during the War - the tank and coal stage was invaluable, for the mechanical coal hoist broke down at intervals and it was an ideal place for engines awaiting some particularly extended repair.

Brunswick shed can be said to have suffered from abysmal siting - almost any shunt of engines involved going out onto the main line, a nagging worry in itself, whilst fires had frequently to be dropped within the shed itself. This was ghastly work, only relieved to some minuscule degree by the notional need to conform with the blackout.

The CLC system escaped relatively lightly in the blitz. Brunswick depot for example, one of the largest railway targets in Liverpool, suffered only superficial damage.

NORTH LIVERPOOL

After its formation the CLC went through a long, lean period, initially because of the recession and subsequently as a result of heavy expenditure on the main line and Liverpool Central extension. However, the Committee in general and the MS&L in particular were envious of the LNWR and L&Y, both of which had depots close to the rapidly expanding northern docks. Brunswick was in no position to capture a share of the vast goods traffic handled at quays beyond the Pier Head, so a branch to north Liverpool was a tempting prospect.

During 1871 a line in a tunnel under the city centre was considered, but the estimated cost was £1.5 million and the idea was abandoned. Incidentally - as noted earlier - the tunnel scheme was resurrected during the 1880s and again dismissed. The MS&L would not rest and in August 1873 insisted that a goods depot in the northern docks, together with a branch line, were essential. The GN declared it would not spend any more money on Merseyside however; it had contributed a third of the capital for the Liverpool lines and was receiving considerably less than a third of the revenue. When an acceptable income was guaranteed, Kings Cross

KING OF KNOTTY ASH

fell in line and the CLC began planning a less expensive line through farmland east of the city.

In anticipation of parliamentary approval, the Committee purchased 25 acres of land near Huskisson Dock, thus gaining a foothold deep in L&Y territory, albeit with no rail access. The CLC North Liverpool Lines Act was passed on 30th July 1874. This sanctioned an eleven mile branch from Hunts Cross on the main line to a terminus at Sandhills and a two and a quarter mile connection from Fazakerley to the L&Y at Aintree. Triangular junctions were to be created by spurs from Hunts Cross East to Halewood North and Fazakerley West to North, both of them less than a mile long. The estimated cost was just over £923,000.

In June 1875 the contract was let and work began two months later. Land purchase had been no problem as much of the route lay through the estate of Lord Derby who was co-operative and sold the required ground for £20,000. Initially the only passenger stations planned were to be at West Derby and Walton on the Hill, but a decision was soon made to provide others at Gateacre, Childwall and Old Swan & Knotty Ash. The last three would merely serve small farming villages and

clearly some residential development was anticipated. The L&Y was approached, to no avail, about building a joint station at Aintree for the races, so the CLC decided to go ahead with its own facilities. Early in 1878 the name Huskisson was adopted instead of Sandhills for the terminus.

On 1st December 1879 the North Liverpool lines from Hunts Cross and Halewood to Walton on the Hill and Aintree opened for goods traffic. A passenger service of a dozen trains each way between Liverpool Central and Walton on the Hill was inaugurated at the same time. Double track was provided throughout and the route, to the east of the sandstone ridge, was a relatively easy one. Minor undulations on the gentle western slopes of the Ditton Brook and River Alt valleys were countered by a succession of earthworks, thus maintaining easy gradients. Modest embankments were a feature from Halewood to Childwall, cuttings took the line past Knotty Ash, and more embankments marked the approach to Walton.

There were no level crossings but numerous bridges, both under and over the track where lanes and roads were encountered. The line crossed several radial routes out of Liverpool - to Widnes, Warrington, St Helens and Ormskirk for example. North of the Fazakerley junctions the L&Y added to CLC expense; in less than a mile no fewer than four bridges were required where the North Liverpool line to Aintree had to cross tracks belonging to its rival. A passenger service from Liverpool Central to Aintree Racecourse station (Aintree from September 1884 and Aintree Central from August 1951) commenced on 13th July 1880. The curve from Fazakerley West Junction to Fazakerley North Junction opened in 1884. North of Aintree, the link to L&Y metals at Aintree Junction seems to have been largely in situ from the outset, but it was not physically connected and brought into use until 1888.

Although probably not appreciated at the time, the passenger stations were pioneering a new architectural fashion. Midland influence was clearly paramount, but the hint of 'Domestic Revival' seen on the North Liverpool line anticipated that company's finest practice by nearly twenty years. The best buildings were at West Derby, on an overbridge carrying Mill Lane, and at Gateacre, approached by a path from Belle Vale Road. They featured broad, low-pitched roofs, tall chimneys and vaguely Tudor windows. Sandstone dressings embellished the brickwork. The same style was seen on a more modest scale at Childwall, but Old Swan & Knotty Ash was quite plain. Aintree had a fairly ordinary station house on Park Lane, virtually next door to the L&Y establishment, but was provided with four through platforms and a bay to cope with Grand National traffic. Old Swan & Knotty Ash became Knotty Ash & Stanley in November 1888.

The two mile extension from Walton on the Hill to Huskisson opened for goods traffic on 1st July 1880, thus completing the North Liverpool lines. Delayed commissioning of this crucial connection to the docks was understandable in view of the engineering work required, for once again the sandstone ridge stood in the way. The line needed to descend at gradients as steep as 1 in 80 to reach Sandhills and required three tunnels and several substantial cuttings.

Immediately beyond Walton on the Hill station the tracks entered Walton Hill tunnel (242 yards) which was followed by a 150 yard rock cutting overlooked by Astor Street and spanned by Liston Street. Then came Breeze Hill tunnel (646 yards) below long-established brick pits on top of the ridge. The bore emerged in a 70 yard cutting overlooked by the back yards of Selwyn Street, residents on the opposite side of this Victorian backwater enjoying views of the LNWR Bootle branch! Beyond Hawthorne Road tunnel (248 yards) the rails ran in a deep cutting alongside Kirkdale station on the L&Y main line. At this point intricate engineering work was necessary where the CLC crossed the deep level Bootle branch (Chapter 1). This sunken course continued alongside the L&Y as far as Huskisson and it required a hefty aqueduct to accommodate the Leeds & Liverpool canal, just short of the terminus.

By 1883 the CLC had spent £150,000 on goods sheds, hydraulic cranes, wharves, offices, a turntable and other facilities at Huskisson, but its growing share of dock traffic was beginning to pay dividends. The investment also included a passenger station in a corner of the vast yard near Boundary Street. This was a fairly rudimentary effort, comprising an island platform with a canopy, but little else in the way of facilities. Services from Liverpool Central via Walton on the Hill commenced on 2nd August 1880, but they were an abject failure and ceased on 1st May 1885. The ever-optimistic MS&L proposed a Preston-Huskisson passenger service a couple of years later, but its CLC partners dismissed the idea because the erstwhile terminus was well established as a cattle dock! Passenger services to Walton on the Hill only lasted until 1st January 1918, although the station was used for excursion trains in subsequent years.

In 1874 the Midland Railway opened a rather fine goods receiving warehouse at Whitechapel in the city centre. It was just over a quarter of a mile from Central station and was never rail served. About the same time the company also established a depot near Sandon Dock, but in this case completion of the Huskisson branch enabled these facilities to be connected to the CLC system. A circuitous link of less than half a mile began on the west side of Huskisson yard and headed first northwards, then westwards, passing beneath the L&Y main line embankment and North Docks branch viaduct in quick succession. After crossing Derby Road it turned southwards, thus forming an inverted 'U', although a reversal was still necessary to reach part of the

Sandon & Canada Dock depot. Rail traffic to and from Huskisson began on 1st November 1882 and a connection with MD&HB tracks opened simultaneously. A huge red brick warehouse was provided by the Midland Railway at Sandon.

Not content with this railhead, the Midland was also eager to tap the northernmost docks. However, the Bootle branch to Alexandra & Langton Dock goods station was a much more expensive undertaking. It extended for two and a quarter miles from Bootle Branch Junction, immediately north of Fazakerley North Junction and opened on 1st June 1885. From the Aintree line it curved westwards and within half a mile crossed the L&Y Bury line, Rice Lane, and the L&Y Preston line on plate girder bridges with abutments of blue brick, a material characteristic of the branch. After passing behind Walton Jail, the track burrowed under Southport Road and sprouted a branch to Linacre gasworks. This was followed by a brick lined cutting spanned by Fernhill Road, then 481 yard Bootle tunnel beneath Marsh Lane and the Leeds & Liverpool canal, and finally another cutting which included a bridge under Marsh Lane & Strand Road station on the L&Y Southport line. Sidings fanned out in a large yard between Rimrose Road and Regent Road.

By this time the CLC was well established in Liverpool and had a healthy share of the growing dock traffic as well as loyal patronage of its fast passenger trains to Manchester. But developments did not stop there. In May 1898 the GCR opened its own goods receiving warehouse

West Derby station looking towards Aintree. The main building in Mill Lane was somewhat grander than the platform shelters. It still exists, having been variously used as a furniture store, greengrocery and latterly an antiques showroom. The small goods yard is visible through the arch. Photograph J Ryan collection.

Aintree Central, looking north, on 5th November 1960 - the final day of services. The train is the combined stock of the last two workings to Aintree, and Stanier 4MT 2-6-4T No 42445 is about to haul the empty 12 coach formation back to Allerton carriage sidings. Photograph J F Ward.

in the city centre at Hood Street, not far from the Midland premises. This was followed in March 1907 by Alexandra & Canada Dock depot which was reached over MD&HB tracks. Bootle goods depot, exclusively for cold storage, opened in April 1907. A forward-looking scheme for connections with the Liverpool Overhead Railway at St Michaels and from Sefton to Seaforth (thus allowing Overhead trains to operate a circular suburban service) never came to fruition, despite receiving parliamentary approval in 1903.

SOUTHPORT, WALTON ... AND NEAR OBLIVION

By the late 1870s Southport had become a thriving seaside resort and a sizeable dormitory town much favoured by Liverpool businessmen. Its growth largely came about because of the coast railway from Exchange, but certain local worthies did not feel any particular gratitude to the L&Y and thought that some competition would be a good idea. In 1878 they approached the CLC and pointed out that the North Liverpool line to Aintree, then under construction, was an ideal springing point for a branch to Southport. The Committee endorsed the project, but was not willing to subscribe any capital. After further deputations in 1880 the CLC set up a separate company and a Bill was prepared.

The Southport & Cheshire Lines Extension Railway acquired its Act on 11th August 1881, although opposition from landowners required it to stop short of Southport at Birkdale. This was finally overcome and the final section to Lord Street terminus was authorised on 18th

August 1882. From a junction with the CLC just north of Aintree station, the 14 mile line ran across reclaimed marshland to Ainsdale, then through sand dunes to the Southport seafront. As a result, it managed to avoid all settlements of any size, thus posing no threat to the L&Y's residential business.

Traffic began on 1st September 1884, the CLC working its protégé for 60% of gross receipts. However, a lack of cash during the final stages of construction meant that the branch was in a fairly basic state and subject to stringent speed restrictions. Nevertheless, a surprisingly generous timetable was operated from the outset. There were nine trains from Southport Lord Street to Liverpool Central and eight services to Manchester, together with a handful of workings to Gateacre and Warrington. Any attempt to compete with the L&Y for regular through traffic between Liverpool and Southport was doomed to failure, for the distance was 31 miles as opposed to only 18 by the direct route. However, the line carried a lot of excursion traffic in summer and was also used by specials for the Southport Flower Show.

Apart from the grand terminus at Southport Lord Street, most stations had large single storey timber buildings, which looked rather forlorn in their windswept surroundings. Altcar & Hillhouse and Sefton & Maghull had grim two storey brick houses with a single storey extension sporting the simplest of canopies. The last-named was the only station in the immediate vicinity of Liverpool, yet even this was fairly remote. Sefton remained a hamlet and residents of nearby Maghull

favoured the frequent Ormskirk-Exchange trains from the L&Y station.

Although the Aintree-Southport branch remained a rather quiet appendage, the North Liverpool line itself became a very busy part of the CLC network. Crucial to the working of the extension was Walton shed, and the following portrait is courtesy of John Ward, from an article compiled for the Great Central Railway Society's magazine, *Forward:*

The depot opened on 13th May 1881 and stood at the western end of Fazakerley triangle, next to Walton on the Hill station. It was unusual in that three companies used the facilities, yet the actual owner had no engines of its own. The shed originally had four roads and was primarily intended for locos engaged on dock shunting, banking from Huskisson to Walton and local goods trips. A much larger shed was built at Allerton in 1882 for servicing incoming main line engines, but it proved an expensive white elephant and was abandoned as a depot during the 1890s. Instead, Walton's role was expanded to cover such duties and the building was enlarged to accommodate six roads in 1885.

The shed also became responsible for long distance workings. For instance, Midland men based at Walton had goods turns to Carlisle, Stourton, Sheffield, Washwood Heath, Nottingham, Burton on Trent and Rowsley. With the grouping of 1923 it became LMS/LNER joint, each company being allocated three roads and having separate offices. The LMS immediately brought in ex-L&Y 0-4-0STs and 0-6-0STs to replace former Midland locos on dock and banking work, although the existing stud of 0-6-0s for goods duties was retained. Six-coupled goods engines of class J10 also featured strongly in the LNER allocation, but there were also several D5 and D8 4-4-0s for the Southport to Liverpool and Manchester passenger trains.

The LMS pulled out during 1936 and its locos were despatched to other sheds. At the dawn of British Railways in 1948, Walton's complement of ex-LNER engines included one D9 4-4-0, one J11 and several J10 0-6-0s, and a couple of N5 0-6-2Ts, although several ex-LMS locos were soon drafted in. At the same time, the range of visiting engines was remarkable. They came regularly from sheds at Gorton, Sheffield, Colwick, Mexborough and Staveley, but occasionally from Hull, Immingham, Tuxford, Darlington, Annesley, Langwith, York, Frodingham, Barnsley, Lincoln, Woodford, Heaton and Ardsley.

Long distance goods trains originating at Huskisson remained a core duty. In summer 1939 there were twenty booked departures to places as diverse as York, King's Cross, Burton on Trent, Birmingham Lawley Street, Whitemoor, Sheffield, Wrexham and Rowsley. There were still twelve main line freight rosters for Walton as late as 1959 - to York (2), Rowsley (2), Dewsnap (2), Amberswood, Cheadle, Spinkhill, Colwick, Sheffield and Long Meg. The Colwick train conveyed imported tobacco for Players at Nottingham and the Long Meg train consisted of empty anhydrite wagons returning to the Settle & Carlisle line from Widnes via Halewood, Aintree, Preston and Hellifield.

Once a year, usually towards the end of March, the North Liverpool line handled a large amount of excursion traffic for the Grand National, with Walton depot servicing the locos. There were 29 trains in 1905 and thirty each year from 1928 to 1939. The highlight in pre-World War 2 days was an Al Pacific on the train from King's Cross. Traffic never reached these levels after the war, but there was still plenty of variety. In 1948 the eight workings included trains from Doncaster and Bristol, whilst 1950 saw excursions from Skegness, Cleethorpes, Colchester, Peterborough and Nottingham.

1956 was a typical year, the departures from Aintree Central for the journey home being as follows: 4.55pm Glasgow St Enoch (40657/45438); 5.05pm St Albans (11144/44753); 5.13pm Barrow/Carlisle (45583 ASSAM); 5.20pm Manchester (45006); 5.30pm Birmingham (44919); 5.37pm Manchester (41066); 5.45pm Newark Castle (44861); 5.56pm Cleethorpes (61265); 6.05pm Scunthorpe (61161). From 1960 there were only six Grand National trains a year over the North Liverpool line and these finished in 1963.

Walton's freight duties declined sharply in the early 1960s, although it still

played host to visiting engines. Passenger work also went with the cut back of services on the North Liverpool line, but two 2-6-4Ts were still allocated at the end. Closure came on 15th December 1963 and the site is now a housing estate.

As noted earlier, the CLC withdraw passenger trains between Walton on the Hill and Huskisson on 1st May 1885. This was against a background of an expanding railway system, but with far more convenient services from nearby stations the Committee was over-optimistic to introduce them in the first place. Otherwise, its Liverpool network thrived while there was plenty of traffic on offer, but during the 1960s complete annihilation of the former CLC became a distinct possibility.

St James (the first station out of Central) and Sefton & Maghull (on the Southport line) had closed on 1st January 1917 as a result of wartime economies. The former never reopened; the once fashionable areas above its dingy platforms had declined and trams satisfied local needs. Regular passenger services returned to the latter on 1st April 1919, although the whole branch had opened up for Grand National racegoers a few days before - no doubt this helped lift the gloom! Meanwhile Walton on the Hill station closed for ever on 1st January 1918 - apart from the occasional excursion.

The LMS adopted a positive attitude to the North Liverpool line and provided two new stations in the eastern suburbs. Clubmoor opened on 14th April 1927; serving a new housing development, it stood adjacent to Broad Lane and boasted a neat stone-built shelter on each platform. Warbreck station near Walton Vale welcomed its first passengers on 1st August 1929 and had little brick shelters on the side platforms, but trains only called during the summer. Unfortunately there was a negative side as well. Childwall,one of the original stations, closed on 1st January 1931. It had remained as remote as when it opened, merely serving six railway houses, a farm and a solitary dwelling. The next nearest housing was half a mile away up a steep hill and their occupants had convenient buses to the city centre. Goods facilities, consisting of a short siding, were withdrawn on 6th August 1943, a remarkably early casualty. A large council estate was built at Childwall in the mid-1950s, but the station stayed closed.

During World War 2 the North Liverpool line played a vital role, for it was well clear of the heavily bombed parts of the city and maintained an essential link to the docks. A constant procession of secretive goods trains consisting of vans and well-sheeted wagons rumbled through suburban Gateacre as other routes were put out of action. In Bootle the CLC was less fortunate; the former GCR Alexandra & Canada Dock warehouse was destroyed in the blitz.

When British Railways inherited the CLC in 1948 the pre-grouping infrastructure was virtually intact, but retrenchment imminent. Otterspool station on the original Garston & Liverpool line was still well away from housing developments and it closed on 5th March 1951. Similarly, Halewood on the Manchester line had few customers and facilities were withdrawn on 17th September 1951. The Southport line had been hopelessly uneconomic for some time and passenger trains between Lord Street and Aintree Central finished on 7th January 1952. Excursions to Southport Chapel Street contiued to run over the North Liverpool Extension until July 1966, travelling via Aintree Junction and the former L&Y route through Burscough. Goods workings ceased on the same date in 1952, though private sidings traffic at Altcar & Hillhouse sustained a link from the southern end for another eight years. The sparse Aintree Central-Liverpool Central passenger service was cut back to Gateacre on 7th November 1960, resulting in the closure of the already-moribund Aintree Central, Warbreck, Clubmoor, West Derby and Knotty Ash & Stanley stations. As mentioned previously, Aintree Central was used on Grand National days until 1963.

Goods facilities on the former CLC lines disappeared steadily over a ten year period. West Derby yard closed on 1st June 1964, Garston followed on 7th September, and Aintree Central finished on 7th December. Gateacre lost its sidings on 4th December 1965 and Walton on the Hill yard went on 9th September 1968. The short branch to Sandon Dock ceased to operate on 24th February 1969, followed by the line to Langton Dock on 5th January 1970. Brunswick goods closed in April 1971, sidings at Knotty Ash & Stanley became redundant on 1st May 1972, and the depot at Wavertree & Edge Hill, deep in former LNWR territory, ceased to accept public traffic on 3rd September 1973, although private sidings continued until 1976.

Meanwhile, after much delay caused by difficulties providing alternative bus services, the Liverpool Central - Gateacre diesel railcars ceased on 17th April 1972. In addition to the city centre and suburban termini, intermediate stations at St Michaels, Mersey Road & Aigburth, Cressington & Grassendale and Garston closed on that day. Trains to Manchester and elsewhere had used Lime Street and the spur at Allerton for some time. The North Liverpool line from Hunts Cross to Huskisson yard was officially taken out of use on 11th February 1979, although traffic at the dock terminus had ceased towards the end of 1978, just short of its centenary.

Fortunately it is possible to end on a brighter note. Merseyrail reopened the line south of Liverpool Central, together with stations at St Michaels, Aigburth, Cressington and Garston on 3rd January 1978. The terminus itself was not reinstated of course, as the Northern Line burrowed beneath the city centre from Moorfields and came in some way along Great George Street tunnel. Electric trains were subsequently extended from Garston to Hunts Cross, so it is once again possible to travel by a through train from the southern suburbs to Southport - albeit via a wholly different route. A new station opened at Halewood on 16th May 1988, about a third of a mile west of the original site. It is now possible to explore the North Liverpool line at leisure, for the former railway has been converted into a footpath and cycleway.

DEPARTURES FROM LIVERPOOL CENTRAL
Monday to Saturday, July 1960
SO - Saturdays Only
SX - Saturdays Excepted
Liverpool Central was much busier than this timetable suggests because of the departures for James Street and the Wirral from Central Low Level, although this was a completely separate operation.
5.05am Stockport Tiviot Dale (via Northenden)
5.45am Manchester Central
6.13am Manchester Central
6.30am Tanhouse Lane (Widnes)
6.35am Gateacre
7.00am Warrington Central
7.12am Manchester Central
7.30am Manchester Central
7.35am Warrington Central
7.42am Gateacre
8.06am Warrington Central
8.30am Manchester Central
8.50am Gateacre
9.12am Warrington Central
9.25am SO Doncaster
9.30am Hull (Buffet Car)
9.42am Gateacre
10.12am Warrington Central
10.30am Stockport Tiviot Dale (via Manchester Central)
10.42am Gateacre
11.12am Warrington Central
11.30am Manchester Central
11.42am Gateacre
11.55am SO Manchester Central
12.00 noon Stockport Tiviot Dale (via Northenden)
12.07pm SO Gateacre
12.12pm SX Warrington Central
12.20pm SO Warrington Central
12.30pm Stockport Tiviot Dale (via Manchester Central)
12.42pm Gateacre
12.50pm SO Cambridge (via Manchester Central, Sheffield Victoria, Lincoln Central, Spalding Town)
12.55pm Warrington Central
1.15pm Harwich Parkeston Quay (via Manchester Central, Sheffield Victoria, Lincoln Central, Spalding Town; connects with night sailing to Hook of Holland; Res-

taurant Car from Sheffield Victoria)
1.30pm Manchester Central
1.42pm Gateacre
2.12pm Warrington Central
2.30pm Nottingham Midland (via Manchester Central, Stockport Tiviot Dale)
2.42pm Gateacre
3.12pm Warrington Central
3.30pm Stockport Tiviot Dale (via Manchester Central)
3.42pm Gateacre
4.12pm Warrington Central
4.30pm SX Manchester Central
4.30pm SO Leicester Central
4.42pm Gateacre
4.52pm Hull (Buffet Car)
4.56pm Stockport Tiviot Dale (via Northenden)
5.00pm SX Warrington Central
5.12pm SO Warrington Central
5.35pm SX Aintree Central
5.40pm SX Warrington Central
5.42pm SO Gateacre
5.50pm SX Gateacre
6.12pm Warrington Central
6.30pm Manchester Central
6.42pm Gateacre
7.12pm Warrington Central
7.30pm Manchester Central
7.42pm Gateacre
8.12pm Warrington Central
8.20pm Manchester Central
8.42pm Gateacre
9.12pm Warrington Central
9.30pm London Marylebone
9.42pm Gateacre
10.10pm Stockport Tiviot Dale (via Manchester Central)
10.30pm Hunts Cross
10.50pm Manchester Central
11.12pm Hunts Cross

BRUNSWICK (8E) SHED ALLOCATION JANUARY 1954

Ex-LMS Stanier 3MT 2-6-2T: 40093, 40118, 40127, 40203
Ex-LMS Compound 4P 4-4-0: 41116, 41118, 41151
Ex-LMS Fowler 4MT 2-6-4T: 42349, 42352
Ex-LMS Stanier 4MT 2-6-4T: 42448. 42466, 42479, 42584, 42597, 42598, 42612, 42628, 42664
Ex-LMS Stanier 5MT 2-6-0: 42949
Ex-LMS 4F 0-6-0: 44396, 44489, 44494
Ex-LMS Stanier 5MT 4-6-0: 45217, 45333, 45346
Ex-LMS 3F 0-6-0T: 47309, 47320, 47327, 47566
Ex-GCR Pollitt(*)/Robinson(+) J10 0-6-0: 65142*, 65145*, 65147*, 65166*, 65182+, 65185+, 65196+
Ex-Great Eastern J67(*)/J69(+) 0-6-0T: 68547*, 68559+
Ex-MS&L Parker N5 0-6-2T: 69254, 69258, 69272
Total allocation 41

WALTON (27E) SHED ALLOCATION JANUARY 1954
Ex-LMS Fairburn 4MT 2-6-4T: 42111, 42112, 42113
Ex-LMS 4F 0-6-0: 44038, 44218, 44481, 44541
Ex-L&Y Aspinall 2F 0-6-0ST: 51338
Ex-GCR Pollitt(*)/Robinson(+) J10 0-6-0: 65133*, 65177+, 65180+, 65192+
Ex-Great Eastern J69 0-6-0T: 68585
Ex-MS&L Parker N5 0-6-2T: 69265, 69298, 69344, 69356
Total allocation 17

Seen from the first coach of a Liverpool University Passenger Transport Society railtour on 13th June 1964, 'Jinty' 0-6-0T No 47487 ambles down towards Huskisson. The train is about to pass over the former LNWR Bootle branch which is in a deep cutting here, and the portal of the tunnel where it burrowed under Kirkdale station on the L&Y main line can be seen behind the platelayer's hut.

Huskisson goods yard, looking south, on 15th July 1952. The angular metal structure in the left background is one of the pylons carrying electricity cables above the Leeds & Liverpool canal. Huskisson passenger station was in the far corner of the yard, just below the prominent white factory.

'Jinty' 0-6-0T No 47487 with a Liverpool University railtour at Huskisson, a location not normally available to enthusiasts. The prominent signal box is Sandhills No 2 on the ex-L&Y main line out of Exchange. This view was taken on 13th June 1964.

A good impression of the massive engineering work on the Midland Railway branch from Bootle Branch Junction to Langton Dock. The tunnel in the foreground was beneath the L&Y Southport line and Marsh Lane & Strand Road station, whilst the bridge in the background carried Stanley Road. Another tunnel, out of sight round the distant curve, burrowed below Linacre gasworks. The view was taken during the 1930s. Photograph D Ibbotson.

Dock, Mersey & Overhead Railways

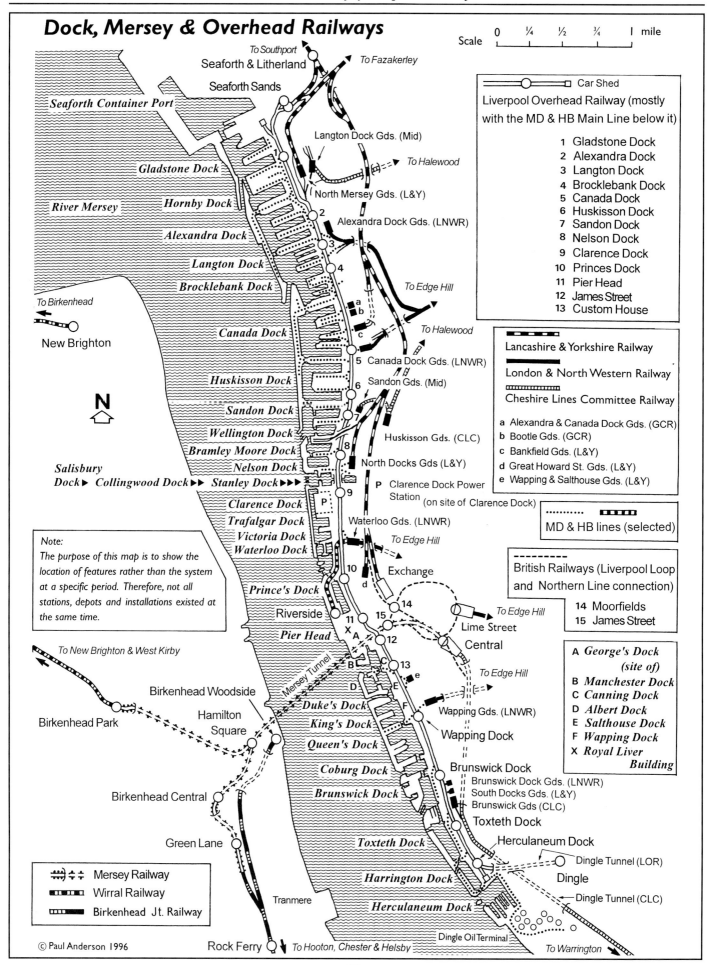

Scale 0 ¼ ½ ¾ 1 mile

Liverpool Overhead Railway (mostly with the MD & HB Main Line below it)

1 Gladstone Dock
2 Alexandra Dock
3 Langton Dock
4 Brocklebank Dock
5 Canada Dock
6 Huskisson Dock
7 Sandon Dock
8 Nelson Dock
9 Clarence Dock
10 Princes Dock
11 Pier Head
12 James Street
13 Custom House

Lancashire & Yorkshire Railway
London & North Western Railway
Cheshire Lines Committee Railway

a Alexandra & Canada Dock Gds. (GCR)
b Bootle Gds. (GCR)
c Bankfield Gds. (L&Y)
d Great Howard St. Gds. (L&Y)
e Wapping & Salthouse Gds. (L&Y)

MD & HB lines (selected)

British Railways (Liverpool Loop and Northern Line connection)
14 Moorfields
15 James Street

A *George's Dock (site of)*
B *Manchester Dock*
C *Canning Dock*
D *Albert Dock*
E *Salthouse Dock*
F *Wapping Dock*
X *Royal Liver Building*

Note:
The purpose of this map is to show the location of features rather than the system at a specific period. Therefore, not all stations, depots and installations existed at the same time.

Mersey Railway
Wirral Railway
Birkenhead Jt. Railway

© Paul Anderson 1996

Features labelled on map:

To Southport
Seaforth & Litherland
To Fazakerley
Seaforth Sands
Seaforth Container Port
Gladstone Dock
Langton Dock Gds. (Mid)
River Mersey
Hornby Dock
To Halewood
North Mersey Gds. (L&Y)
Alexandra Dock
Alexandra Dock Gds. (LNWR)
Langton Dock
Brocklebank Dock
To Edge Hill
To Birkenhead
Canada Dock
New Brighton
To Halewood
Canada Dock Gds. (LNWR)
Sandon Gds. (Mid)
Huskisson Dock
Huskisson Gds. (CLC)
Sandon Dock
Wellington Dock
North Docks Gds (L&Y)
Bramley Moore Dock
Nelson Dock
Salisbury Dock ▶ *Collingwood Dock* ▶▶ *Stanley Dock* ▶▶▶
Clarence Dock
Clarence Dock Power Station (on site of Clarence Dock)
Trafalgar Dock
Victoria Dock
Waterloo Gds. (LNWR)
Waterloo Dock
To Edge Hill
Exchange
Prince's Dock
Riverside
Moorfields
To Edge Hill
Lime Street
Central
Pier Head
James Street
Mersey Tunnel
To Edge Hill
Birkenhead Woodside
Hamilton Square
Duke's Dock
Wapping Gds. (LNWR)
Birkenhead Park
Wapping Dock
King's Dock
Birkenhead Central
Queen's Dock
Coburg Dock
Brunswick Dock Gds. (LNWR)
South Docks Gds. (L&Y)
Green Lane
Brunswick Dock
Brunswick Gds (CLC)
Toxteth Dock
Herculaneum Dock
Toxteth Dock
Dingle Tunnel (LOR)
Dingle
Harrington Dock
Tranmere
Dingle Tunnel (CLC)
Herculaneum Dock
To Warrington
Rock Ferry ▼ To Hooton, Chester & Helsby
Dingle Oil Terminal
To New Brighton & West Kirby

CHAPTER 4

MERSEY MISCELLANY

Liverpool Corporation AEC Regent A356 heads into James Street on route 87 to Garston as a Seaforth - Dingle train rumbles towards James Street station. In this 14th April 1955 view, the Dock Office forms an impressive backdrop. Photograph R.B. Parr.

As outlined in previous chapters, the LNWR, L&Y and CLC were basically radial routes from the centre of Liverpool, although all three concerns reached the docks by means of branches. However, the Mersey and its miles of quays gave rise to three local railways not directly associated with the main line companies. In fact two of them remained independently owned until closure, whilst the third only lost its separate identity when nationalised in 1948. There could not have been a greater contrast between them, and in turn they had a wholly different character to the routes out of Lime Street, Exchange and Central.

The first was the Mersey Docks and Harbour Board system serving quays, warehouses, yards and factories from Gladstone Dock to Dingle. A railway along the dock road was resisted initially, but it soon became desirable and eventually proved essential to the commerce of the port. Although saddle tanks trundling through the streets lacked the glamour of main line departures from Lime Street and were certainly nowhere near as swift as electric suburban trains out of Exchange, they had an air all their own.

The second Mersey railway was literally that - the Mersey Railway from Central Low Level to the Wirral. It tunnelled beneath the river and was largely out of sight, although James Street station certainly made its presence felt by the tall tower essential for hydraulic operation of the lift. The line broke new ground in two ways: it was the first to

run through a deep level tunnel in an urban area, and the conversion from steam to electric traction was a truly pioneering venture.

Most abandoned railways soon fade in the memory as far as the general public is concerned, but occasionally one becomes part of local and even national folklore. This is certainly the case with the Liverpool Overhead which closed forty

years ago, leaving few traces. The 'Dockers' Umbrella' ran almost entirely on a metal gantry affording visitors exhilarating views of the teeming docks. It earned its living by carrying those with business in the port - from workers with broad Scouse accents to mariners speaking the tongues of a hundred seafaring nations. There was no equivalent in Britain to the lightweight electric trains which ran every

Former L&Y 0-4-0ST No.51206 crossing the tram tracks at the junction of James Street, Goree and Mann Island as it plods north along the dock line with wagons from Wapping Dock Goods. In this 1954 view the train is preceded by 'a man with a red flag' as usual, while Liverpool Corporation AEC Regent A774 waits patiently. The MD&HB, Mersey Railway and Overhead lines came together at this point, albeit isolated from each other. Trains between Central Low Level and the Wirral were in the tunnel well below street level. The smoke deflector on the 'pug' is clearly not very effective and it is easy to see how sixty years of this treatment corroded the Overhead decking. Photograph J.F. Ward Collection.

Ex-L&Y 'Pug' No.51232 is stoked up between duties at Wapping Dock. This evocative view, taken on 29th October 1960, shows the severe track curvature which demanded short wheelbase locomotives. Photograph J.A. Peden.

Avonside 0-6-0ST No.1, dating from 1904, holds up road traffic near the entrance to North Mersey Goods Yard on 21st May 1962. This MD&HB loco is now preserved in the Merseyside County Museum. Photograph A. Swain.

few minutes from Dingle to Seaforth and back.

The three subjects of this chapter equate to a trio of highly evocative books by John W. Gahan entitled *Rails to Port and Starboard*, *The Line Beneath the Liners* and *Seventeen Stations to Dingle*. Only a glimpse of the Mersey Docks and Harbour Board system, the Mersey Railway and Liverpool Overhead is possible in a book of this nature, so readers wishing to delve further and absorb the atmosphere of the city's very own railways are strongly recommended to consult these local works.

THE DOCK LINES

In everyday parlance, the long thoroughfare from Seaforth to Dingle which separated the commercial and residential ar-

eas of Liverpool from the docks was known as the Dock Road, yet not a single stretch of it actually bore this name. Instead, this vital artery comprised (from north to south) Regent Road, Waterloo Road, Bath Street, New Quay, Georges Dock Gate, Goree, Strand Street, Wapping, Chaloner Street and Sefton Street. Despite this apparent fragmentation, there was a common thread for over a century - the MD&HB 'main line'.

Even in the 1950s when the docks were facing an uncertain future, sturdy saddle tanks seemed to rule the streets as if nothing was amiss. With their bells tolling continuously and a man holding a red flag walking in front, the engines trundled strings of wagons between quay and warehouse. At the Pier Head and James Street they delayed trams, buses, lorries

and cars with disdain. Here, as elsewhere, the dock locos ran beneath the Overhead Railway, blasting the structure with generous doses of sulphurous smoke. Having progressed so far along the 'main line', they veered sharply away from massive warehouses on the Dock Road and entered a world of transit sheds, cranes and cargo ships, wheel flanges on the wagons squealing in protest.

When the Liverpool & Manchester reached Wapping in 1830, the port was still very compact. Seven docks extended for about a mile and a half, the centre of activity being the lively and often raucous area around Canning Place. To the south, the shoreline stretched away past the sandstone bluff at Dingle to Knotts Hole and the Grassendale estate. To the north lay the sand dunes of Bootle Bay, old forts dating from the time when Liverpool was in danger of attack from the sea, and three country houses - Stanley Hall, Miller's Castle and Seaforth Hall. By 1850 Jesse Hartley had built thirteen additional docks, and the commercial waterfront now stretched for over three miles.

The first hint of a dock railway system came in 1835 when the Liverpool & Manchester was given permission to lay a siding from Wapping goods depot to the east side of King's Dock, and this materialised in 1844. A year later, Hartley advised the Dock Trustees that a line along the Dock Road with branches to various quays was a necessary development. Previously, such a proposal would have been unthinkable but the authorities had begun to acknowledge the increasing role of railways in the movement of goods nationally. Their decision was favourable and track soon appeared in the cobbled streets.

By 1848 rails stretched from Wapping depot, past Custom House, James Street and Georges Pier Head to the new Stanley Dock. Three years later, the 'main line' reached south to Toxteth Dock and in 1852 there was an extension northwards when Huskisson Dock opened. Branches were gradually laid to serve individual sources of traffic - Brunswick Dock (1852), Canning Dock (1853), Wapping warehouse (1857) and Waterloo LNWR depot (1858), for example. By 1860 the system extended from Canada Dock to Harrington Dock, a distance approaching five miles. Development continued during the 1870s and 1880s when more quays and a few industrial establishments associated with the docks were connected to the MD&HB network.

Occasionally, small tank engines belonging to the LNWR and L&Y ventured on to the dock line with special permission, but otherwise horse traction reigned supreme for nearly half a century. Indeed, from 1852 to the opening of the Liverpool Overhead in 1893, a well patronised horse bus service plied along the street railway. The sheer volume of traffic eventually

VICTORIA TOWER

WAPPING HYDRAULIC TOWER

became too much for equine power and in 1895 the use of steam locomotives was allowed throughout the system. At first contractors' engines were employed, but from 1904 to 1941 the MD&HB purchased a succession of robust Avonside, then Hunslet, 0-6-0 saddle tanks with flangeless centre driving wheels to cope with the sharp curves. They were housed in five sheds - at Hornby Dock, Canada Dock, Huskisson Dock, Princes Dock and Brunswick Dock. Locos from the main line companies regularly used the dock railway for trips between depots, but were not allowed into the docks themselves.

The MD&HB line had largely acquired its distinctive character by 1900 when the Overhead Railway gantry spanned much of the formation and most large goods depots and warehouses along the dock road were in place. However, the development of sidings was surprisingly

sluggish until the system assumed a strategic importance in World War I, when several new branches were laid. At the same time the loco stud increased markedly, and from then on engines seemed to be everywhere in the estate.

Besides plodding along the street, saddle tanks disappeared down dark chasms between towering mill walls, squeezed through gateways into factory yards, simmered in the shadow of great cargo ships, and ventured along remote sea walls shrouded in mist. Lines ran close to Hartley's massive colonnaded warehouses and whimsical grey towers in the older docks and encountered huge angular transit sheds and gaunt silos in the later basins. In the dock road itself there was a backdrop of dour warehouses, ornate railway goods depots, factories and mills, pubs and cafes and the occasional shop. Wagons carried timber, machinery, foodstuffs, coal, cotton and virtually every other commodity imaginable. The tang of smoke produced by locos and ships mingled with other aromas of the port, from spices and tobacco to molasses and grain.

Expansion continued between the wars, new track reaching Dingle oil jetties in 1922, Gladstone Dock during 1927 and both Stanley Dock tobacco warehouse and Clarence Dock Power Station in 1931. Inevitably, the blitz of 1940-41 played havoc with the MD&HB system, but repairs were completed in days or even hours to keep the vital traffic flowing. Nevertheless, some branches were never reinstated, their source of traffic having been totally destroyed.

For a decade of so after the war, freighters and trans-Atlantic liners were

as familiar a sight in the port as they had been prior to 1939. The saddle tanks also scuttled around much as before, although a couple of diesel shunters had joined them. However, by the early 1960s there had been dramatic changes. Container ships were becoming increasingly important, larger vessels had rendered most older docks superfluous, the rise in trade with Europe was favouring east coast ports, airliners had captured most North American passenger traffic and lorries were very much in favour, to the detriment of the MD&HB trains. It was a telling development that acres of former sidings and yards were turned over to container stores, lorry depots and car parks.

During 1961 the section of 'main line' between Princes Dock and Wapping became more or less moribund with the end of trip workings from Park Lane to Huskisson. Afterwards there were only occasional trains past James Street and

MD&HB No.14, a Hunslet 0-6-0ST of 1931, rests between shunts in Regent Road near Brocklebank Dock on 30th September 1959. The Harland & Wolff Engineering Works is in the background and one of the Avonside locos is further down the line. Photograph A. Swain.

On 30th September 1959, Hunslet 0-6-0ST No.11 emerges from Thos. W. Ward's yard and is about to negotiate the sharp curve to the MD&HB main line. The engine was built in 1940 and the somewhat newer Hillman Minx just about avoided a glancing blow! Photograph A. Swain.

the Pier Head, sometimes with many months between them. Another traffic flow was lost when the huge granaries at Alexandra Dock closed in 1965. Five years later the bridge over the entrance to Stanley Dock was taken out, severing the MD&HB system. The very last working past the Pier Head to Salthouse Dock took place during 1971. By the following year, tonnage passing over the Board's railway was just 4% of that carried in the peak years of World War II and complete closure was inevitable. The final train, a trip from Alexandra Dock to the BR yard, ran on 11th September 1973. A contemporary development was the opening of Royal Seaforth Dock north of Bootle, which precipitated the closure of virtually all harbour facilities south of the Pier Head.

Over 100,000 people were employed in the dock area at one time, but by the mid-1970s a significant portion of the estate and its hinterland was deserted and derelict. Tarmac covered most of the erstwhile 'main line' and fragments of sidings led nowhere. Several new warehouses appeared at the southern end of the port, but these were served by road vehicles rather than ships and shunters. In February 1980 there was a slight railway revival when main line diesels began to haul container trains out of Seaforth Terminal along upgraded track connecting with the former LNWR Bootle branch. Four years later Dingle Oil Terminal and Herculaneum Dock were utilised as the site for the Liverpool International Garden Festival and its attendant car park. Undoubtedly the most spectacular development has been the transformation of

Albert Dock into a major tourist attraction, although Hartley's other surviving structures are also receiving attention.

MERSEY RAILWAY

The frequent electric service from numerous stations in the Wirral to Liverpool city centre has been taken for granted for most of this century, and no doubt few people on the trains appreciate the historical significance of the railway beneath the Mersey. It was very much a pioneering venture in construction terms, and the use of steam locomotives on an underground

PIER HEAD BUILDINGS & BIRKENHEAD FERRY

route with severe gradients may be regarded, in retrospect, as adventurous. Another bold move was the decision to electrify the line when that form of traction was in its infancy.

A railway under the river was first mooted in 1864. Although the ferries were well used, they deposited most travellers well short of their destination. The Liverpool & Birkenhead company planned to run trains from Rock Ferry to Brunswick, with the CLC providing onward connec-

tions when its line to Central Station was built. However, the scheme was successfully quashed by the LNWR. A proposed pneumatic railway actually gained parliamentary approval in 1866, but finance was not forthcoming and this idea remained on the drawing board as well. Improved communications with the Cheshire bank was becoming imperative however and in 1869 the Mersey Railway company was formed to build a double track tunnel with conventional steam operation in mind.

An Act of Parliament was secured in 1871, followed by a prolonged gestation period. Excavations for a shaft at Birkenhead soon commenced, but the contractor went out of business and nothing more happened until the end of 1879. This time, 170ft shafts either side of the river were completed as planned and work commenced in 1881 on a pilot tunnel. A start was made on the main tunnel in December of that year and when the headings met beneath the Mersey in January 1884 they were, astonishingly, only one inch out of line! This was the first railway in the world to be built below a tidal estuary and also the first deep level line in an urban area. Naturally, progress was watched with considerable interest both in Britain and abroad.

The original Mersey Railway tracks extended for just under two and a quarter miles from James Street in Liverpool to Green Lane in Birkenhead, 1,320 yards of the route actually being below the river. With a width of 26 feet and a height of 19 feet, the tunnel was a remarkable engineering achievement. It was lined with no less than 38 million bricks and in places they were eight rings deep. The steepest gradient was a punishing 1 in 27 from the centre of the Mersey up to James Street, the climb to Hamilton Square station in Birkenhead being only slightly less severe at 1 in 30. Ancillary drainage and ventilation tunnels were provided. Powerful steam pumping engines kept the railway free of water and huge fans attempted to clear the fumes.

On 20th January 1886 the railway was officially opened by the Prince of Wales on a glittering occasion attended by huge crowds. Regular traffic commenced on 1st February. Because of its fast and frequent service, the line was an immediate success and carried well over 20,000 people on weekdays, the total number of passengers on public holidays sometimes amounting to 50,000. The Mersey Railway reached Birkenhead Park and Rock Ferry on the Wirral during 1888 and 1891 respectively, whilst on 11th January 1892 an extension from James Street to Central Low Level brought the system into the heart of Liverpool. This half-mile line tunnelled beneath Lord Street and Church Street at 1 in 31/34 to reach an island platform directly below the CLC terminus.

There had been nothing quite like James Street station. With platforms some 50 feet below street level, three huge lifts were essential to move the hoards of passengers using the trains every few minutes in peak periods. Each lift could carry a hundred people and the cages were raised or lowered on massive pistons thrusting from cylinders anchored in a pit 90 feet below rail level. Hydraulic pressure was provided by a reservoir housed at the top of a tower 120 feet above street level, the water being pumped up by steam. This imposing structure gave James Street station its character. Along with the rest of the frontage, it was executed in a crenallated Italianate style by

Sporting well kept lined paintwork, Avonside 0-6-0ST No.21 of 1913 poses at Alexandra Dock on 11th April 1959. Note safety valves on the dome and the battered spark arresting mesh. A long shovel, bent in this particular fashion and carried on the front buffer beam, was a characteristic feature of most MD&HB locos. Another shovel adorns the cab roof. The curve in the left background still existed in 1996 as rail access to Seaforth Coal Terminal and Container Depot, but the enormous grain silos on the far side of Regent Road were demolished in 1992-93. Photograph R.C. Riley.

G.E. Grayson. Corner turrets, and what could have been mistaken for a belfry, disguised the tank. The four storey main building featured rows of round-headed windows, dormers in the roof, and even bay windows on the first and second floors. A stone plinth and glass canopy completed the facade.

Walls at platform level were finished off with whitewash or glazed white bricks, brightening up the gas-lit gloom and anticipating the familiar character of London's tube stations. James Street remained more or less as built until the surface buildings were destroyed during the blitz of May 1941. The entrance is now a bland opening in a modern seven storey block, and below ground most traces of the Victorian atmosphere have been masked by Merseyrail refurbishment - a

notable exception being the long pedestrian subway to Water Street. However, some of the character of the original Mersey Railway can be enjoyed at Birkenhead Hamilton Square, where the mighty hydraulic tower still dwarfs the entrance building.

Steam engines worked through the tunnel between Birkenhead and Liverpool for seventeen years. Initially, the company purchased eight powerful 0-6-4 side tanks from Beyer Peacock of Manchester. They were the first ever locomotives with this wheel arrangement, six coupled traction being considered essential for the gradients. Ten 2-6-2 tanks in the same gleaming dark green and brown livery followed. At the turn of the century, a journey below the Mersey in bucking, swaying four-wheel coaches was a noisy and almost asphyxiating experience. The crowded trains tore downhill to gain momentum for the climb at the other side and fumes filled every compartment. Numerous travellers returned to the slower but airy ferries, especially in the evening when the railway was at its most foul.

Although these desertions eroded receipts, the main problem for the Mersey Railway was its enormous operating costs - notably the expensive ventilation system. During 1888 the company went into receivership, and despite its heavy usage and undoubted value to Liverpool, the line sunk further into debt. By the mid-1890s the City & South London and Liverpool Overhead had proved that railways could be operated successfully by electricity and the Mersey company acquired powers in 1896 to convert its line to the new form of traction. But capital was not available and the situation became desperate. Shortly afterwards, in a

MB&HB No.25, an Avonside 0-6-0ST dating from 1918, shunts empties along the quayside at Gladstone Dock, around 1950. Photograph J.A. Peden Collection.

Access to the eastbound platform at James Street in the early 1950s, largely unchanged from Mersey Railway steam days apart from the string of cables and contemporary advertisements. The latter extolled the virtues of Rowntree's Fruit Gums, Senior Service, Brylcreem and Trex (as used by Philip Harben!).

rather optimistic attempt to tap new markets, the company began to run through carriages from Liverpool Central Low Level to Corwen, Folkestone and even London Paddington in association with the Great Western Railway.

With good fortune akin to a fairy tale, the Mersey Railway was rescued by George Westinghouse who arrived from the USA in 1899. He was determined to extend his engineering empire to Britain and saw the underground line as a testbed. Over the next couple of years, a generating station was built at Birkenhead to supply the 650 volt DC power, third and fourth rails were installed, a huge amount of soot was removed from the tunnel, James Street and Central Low Level stations enjoyed a sprucing up and the lifts were converted to electric operation.

On 3rd May 1903 the Mersey Railway became the first line in Britain to be converted from steam to electricity. Passengers accustomed to the subterranean smog welcomed the healthier atmosphere, but initially they were disconcerted by the blue flashes and underfloor clunks and bangs which accompanied a journey below the river. At least the whining of traction motors was reassuring. The old four-wheel coaches had slam doors but the much roomier electric stock featured open end platforms with gates in true trans-Atlantic fashion. In fact the new vehicles with their clerestory roofs,

matchboard sides and distinctive bogies were American in virtually every respect. A dark red livery was applied and the Mersey Railway crest incorporating a Liver Bird was prominent in the centre of each car. Extra carriages of a modified design were purchased in 1923, 1925 and 1936. All eighteen steam locomotives were eventually sold for further use. One, No.5 CECIL RAIKES, worked at a Derbyshire colliery until the 1950s and has been preserved.

At the grouping of 1923, the Mersey Railway escaped the clutches of the LMS and remained independent. During the 1920s, pumping operations were converted to electricity and the platform at Central Low Level was widened. In 1938 the former Wirral Railway (by then part of the LMS) was electrified, and compact yet rather bulbous crimson-lake multiple units began to work through services into the heart of Liverpool. The Mersey Railway lost its separate identity when it became part of BR on 1st January 1948, and unfamiliar green paint gradually replaced the dark red hue. New stock, similar in design to the Wirral trains, displaced the venerable American pattern cars between mid-1956 and the summer of 1957.

For over eighty years, the underground line remained very much as built. In peak periods thousands of people used a broad staircase from the concourse of the old CLC terminus or a subway at the corner of Ranelagh Street and Bold Street

to reach the low level station. Trains departed at remarkably frequent intervals and it was often standing room only for the three minute journey to Hamilton Square. But in 1970 the decision was made to embark upon a radical improvement of the inner Liverpool rail system. From James Street a new single track line was created below the city centre, incorporating a station at Moorfields for the commercial district, another at Lime Street for the main line, and a third at Central for the principal shopping area. The Liverpool Loop ran entirely in a concrete-lined tunnel and it returned to the existing route before James Street. Construction work began in February 1971 and services commenced on 9th May 1977. Central Low Level became part of the Northern Line (see Chapter 2), a section of the original Mersey Railway alignment between Paradise Street and James Street being retained for interchanging stock. This bold venture proved a huge success and patronage of the trains increased by almost a third. Services are now operated by modern electric sets of classes 507 and 508.

LIVERPOOL OVERHEAD

The elevated railway from Dingle to Seaforth Sands was an institution. Together with the 'Green Goddess' trams it is remembered with intense affection by older Liverpudlians - a symbol of more prosperous days when the port was a hive of activity. The line was taken for granted and, indeed, still carried an average of nearly 25,000 passengers a day during its final year of operation.

Being unique in Britain, the Overheard has enjoyed plenty of attention from writers. In additional to John Gahan's book mentioned earlier, *The Liverpool Overhead Railway* by C.E. Box (*Railway World*, London, 1959) and *The Dockers' Umbrella* by Paul Bolger (The Bluecoat Press, Liverpool, 1992) have covered the line admirably. Although there is little new to say, a brief history of the Overhead is essential here, and extracts from *Seventeen Stations to Dingle* have been included by kind permission of John Gahan.

New York's Manhatten Elevated or Bowery of 1870 was the first overhead railway in the world and Britain's pioneering electric line was the City & South London tube, opened in 1890. Credit for the earliest overhead electric railway goes to Liverpool however. A four mile elevated route from Huskisson to Toxteth along the dock road was first mooted in 1852 but nothing come of the idea. The scheme was revived in 1877 by the MD&HB and after research in New York an Act for a single track line was acquired the following year. This was modified to a double track, steam-worked overhead railway from Alexandra to Herculaneum by an Act of 1882. The Dock Board then decided to hand the project over to an independent company, and the Liverpool Overhead Railway was incorporated on 24th July 1888.

Work began in October 1889 with the establishment of a yard alongside the L&Y North Mersey goods depot, for fabricating the girders and deck. At the time, steam traction was still envisaged but the reliability of the City & South London and factors such as lighter axle weight, reduced fire risk and general cleanliness convinced the company that electric traction would be best. Construction proceeded from north to south. Girders, made of steel channels bolted back to back, formed the uprights. They stood 16 feet high and were placed 22 feet apart, allowing room for the double track MD&HB main line which was upgraded and realigned, at considerable expense to the Overhead company. Although a span of 50 feet was considered ideal, two thirds of the deck sections were non-standard, varying from 30 feet to 70 feet. The decking itself rested on wrought iron girders and consisted of arched plates riveted to T bars, forming a light yet strong bed for the track and a watertight roof for the MD&HB line hence its nickname 'Dockers' Umbrella'.

Lift bridges were provided at Langton, Sandon and Brunswick to allow high loads access to the docks. There were also three 98 feet bowstring girder bridges across wide roads, one at James Street and two at the Pier Head. The most expensive single structure was a double deck combined swing and lift bridge where the Overhead and MD&HB line crossed the entrance to Stanley Dock, the only basin east of the dock road. Between Nelson and Huskisson, the elevated tracks dipped to street level so as to pass beneath the High Level Coal Railway. Standard gauge track was pinned to longitudinal sleepers and current came from a central conductor rail.

The five mile line originally had thirteen stations: Alexandra Dock, Brocklebank Dock, Canada Dock, Sandon Dock, Clarence Dock, Princes Dock, Pier Head, James Street, Custom House, Wapping Dock, Brunswick Dock, Toxteth Dock and Herculaneum Dock. Most were fairly basic affairs with 120ft platforms, small timber shelters and staircases down to street level. Pier Head and Custom House were expected to be the busiest and received more attention. They had additional stairways and full length canopies with end screens, virtually forming an overall roof.

Public services commenced on 6th March 1893, although the official opening ceremony had been a month earlier, on 4th February. This was performed by the Marquis of Salisbury who pointed out that the line was the first to be controlled by automatic electric signals. He also predicted (wrongly, as it turned out) that the Overhead would be emulated by other British cities. Fifteen two-car trains with varnished teak bodies were built by Brown, Marshall & Co. (later Metro-Cammell) in Birmingham ready for the start of operations, and a further four were delivered during 1893. In the first year, 4 million passengers were carried.

Even during construction, it was realised that the Overhead would be too dependent on dock workers for its income, and permission to extend into residential areas was acquired in 1892. The northern extension from Alexandra Dock to Seaforth Sands was slightly less than a mile, although it utilised existing tracks to the carriage sheds and new construction amounted to just 342 yards of viaduct. This incorporated a fourth bowstring bridge and terminated at a two-platform terminus with an overall roof. Services commenced on 30th April 1894.

The southern extension from Herculaneum to Dingle was much more adventurous, despite its modest length of

1,087 yards. It veered eastwards just short of Herculaneum terminus which was replaced by a through station and became a second car shed. A 200ft lattice girder bridge carried the Overhead across part of the CLC Brunswick goods yard before the track plunged into Dingle tunnel. This was drilled for half a mile through sandstone and difficult clay bands below a residential area. Sixty yards from the portal the bore encountered the CLC Dingle tunnel a mere three feet below it, and a complex arch at an acute angle had to be constructed to take the weight of Overhead trains. Dingle terminus, consisting of a 170ft island platform and stairs leading to an overbridge, was built in a 52ft wide section of tunnel, the widest in Britain at the time. An inclined subway led to the rather ornate brick station building on Park Road. This stretch of line opened on 21st December 1896.

Even without the southern extension, over 7 million passengers used the Liverpool Overhead during 1896. More rolling stock was imperative, so a further fifteen two-car trains and eight three-car sets were ordered in 1896/97. At the same time more stations were provided. Langton Dock opened in 1896, although it only lasted until 5th March 1906. Sandon Dock closed in 1896, when adjacent stations opened at Huskisson and Nelson.

During 1900, ten million journeys were made on the line, the southern extension having come into its own. But a year later, the railway suffered a disaster. On 23rd December 1901 the heavily used 5pm from Seaforth to Dingle had battled against a gale for half an hour and its traction motors were seriously overheating when it entered the tunnel. The three-car set came to a standstill 80 yards from the platform at Dingle when the motors cut out. Foolishly the driver tried to re-start them three times causing intense arcing which set the coaches on fire. Fanned by a strong draught down the tunnel, the train and station became a roaring inferno. Six people died, including the driver, and the terminus remained closed until early 1903.

By 1900 the newly electrified Liverpool Corporation trams were operating a service from Pier Head to Seaforth Sands in direct competition with the Overhead, and this partly stimulated a number of developments on the railway. In 1900 the company opened a street tramway from Seaforth to Crosby and during 1901 an escalator was installed at Seaforth Sands, anticipating those on the London Underground. 1902/3 saw five two-car trains rebuilt with wider bodywork to accommodate three plus two seating, in hopes of relieving overcrowding at busy periods. Powers were acquired for a connection from Herculaneum to St. Michaels on the CLC in 1903 and these were followed by authority to build the Seaforth

James Street station at 4.20pm, the beginning of the evening rush hour, on a working day some time in the early 1950s. Commuters await trains for the Rock Ferry, New Brighton and West Kirby lines and sales of the evening paper from one of the three kiosks seem to be brisk.

MD&HB Fireless locomotive No.43, built by Andrew Barclay in 1918, at Dingle Oil Terminal on 11th September 1955. The photograph shows why a conventional steam loco could not be used at such locations. Sister engine No 44 was destroyed during an air raid in June 1941. Photograph B. Mettam.

& Sefton Junction Light Railway in 1904. Together, they would have enabled a circular service to operate via Gateacre, Aintree and the Pier Head, but no work was done. The so-called 'Belt Route' later had another abortive airing, this time involving the L&Y North Mersey branch and an extension from Dingle to St. Michaels.

Nevertheless, a short section of new bridgework and far-reaching suburban services did materialise. An extension beyond Seaforth Sands terminus connected with the trackbed of a previously-lifted L&Y branch from Seaforth & Litherland to the North Mersey goods line. It opened on 2nd July 1905. A through station at Seaforth Sands was brought into use at the same time. The Overhead was then equipped with an outside conductor rail, enabling specially-built lightweight L&Y stock to operate hourly between Southport and Dingle. In 1906 a short connection with the parallel North Mersey branch was made at Rimrose Road Junction and L&Y trains began to run between Dingle and Aintree. The Southport workings ceased in 1913 and the Aintree service was confined to race days after World War I.

In 1919 patronage peaked at 17 million journeys per annum. There were about two hundred trains each way on weekdays and the overall timing was four minutes better than early Edwardian days, another response to tram competition. In 1925 the old terminus at Seaforth Sands closed to passengers and was rebuilt as a car shed. The last tram to Crosby ran at the end of the same year. However, on 16th June 1930 a new station was provided at Gladstone Dock. By 1936 all trains were three-car sets. Unfortunately the Depression had bitten with a vengeance; in 1933 less than 6 million passengers used the trains.

Then came the blitz - and the Overhead was in the thick of it. Between the first heavy raid on 21st August 1940 and the last serious attack on 8th May 1941, the elevated structure was damaged fourteen times. Spans were blown away by direct hits, warehouse walls collapsed on the decking, fires buckled the girders, James Street station was completely wrecked and the MALAKAND explosion shattered a considerable length of the railway at Huskisson. Considering that the worst of the dockland blazes could be seen *fifty miles away* in North Wales, it is amazing that the Overhead survived at all. Fortunately, neither car shed was hit, as the provision of specialised replacement vehicles would probably have been out of the question. The line was fully reopened on 1st November 1941. Custom House station became Canning in 1945, the building from which it took its name having been reduced to rubble some years earlier.

From 1945 to 1955 the company rebuilt eight of its trains. The bodywork exterior featured aluminium panelling painted in two shades of brown, sliding doors were provided, and modern seating, lighting and fittings installed. The moquette first class and leather second class seats were a considerable improvement on the old black cloth and wooden seats, but the overall appearance was somewhat bland compared with the original Victorian design.

Most railways on Merseyside were nationalised in 1948, but the Liverpool Overhead escaped the clutches of BR. It remained proudly independent and by means of huge signs on stations and bridges emphasised that it was *the* way of seeing the docks and liners. Tourists flocked to the line and countless school parties from the North and Midlands had incomparable geography and history lessons aboard the rattling trains. A wonderfully evocative description of the journey from Dingle to Seaforth around 1948 is contained in John Gahan's *Seventeen Stations to Dingle*. The following is adapted from that account: '*After purchas-*

Liverpool Central Low Level on 18th February 1965 with trains of second generation electric stock just visible in the gloom. The High Level terminus is directly above the massive girders, resting on excavated sandstone.

Another bowstring girder crossed the junction at St. Nicholas Place, New Quay and Georges Dock Gate, just north of Pier Head Station. A Dingle - Seaforth train crosses it in March 1956. The dock entrance to the Mersey road tunnel can be seen in the background. Photograph S. Creer.

ing our tickets just inside the cinema-like entrance to the station on Park Road, we walk down the subway and stairs leading to the dank and gloomy island platform at Dingle. Before long, one of the old three-car sets arrives with a sigh of air brakes and a handful of passengers slam the doors after boarding it. The compressor bursts into life with a tonk-tonk as pressure is built up in the brake reservoirs. Soon the train begins to roll, slamming and groaning over the points before its half mile run through the tunnel. Sounds from the motor and gears are magnified in the narrow confines and blue flashes emanate from the collector shoes.

'Emerging into the daylight, we cross the girder bridge over the former CLC yard and a splendid view of the Mersey opens up. At Herculaneum we can see several Elder Dempster ships in the docks. The station stop is brief and we are soon passing the massive CLC warehouse on the approach to Toxteth. Brunswick station reveals glimpses of Harrison Lane and Isle of Man Steam Packet cargo vessels whilst a view of the brown bulk of Liverpool Cathedral opens up on the landward side. The wheels beat out a rhythm on the short rail lengths and occasionally a cloud of steam billows up from a MD&HB loco on the line below us. Workshops, ships chandlers, pubs, snack bars, tobacconists and small clothing factories alongside the dock road pass rapidly as we rattle towards Canning and James Street.

'The world famous Dock Board, Cunard and Royal Liver buildings obscure the river as we reach Pier Head station. Several dock workers join or leave the carriage, salutations such as 'Ullo Whack', 'Whereareyerwerkinlads?' or 'Tarrah' being expressed loudly. Matches are struck on the floor, windows or boot soles to light pipes and cigarettes, then the back page of the Echo is scanned to glean the latest news about Everton or Liverpool with a view to exchange scathing witticisms.

'At Princes Dock we see ships engaged in Belfast and Dublin trade, then Bibby's massive seed mill appears on the right. Victoria and Trafalgar Docks are occupied by smaller vessels, and they are followed by Clarence Dock Power Station where locos fuss about with steel hopper wagons. The immense Stanley Dock tobacco warehouse looms up on the landward side before the coach wheels clatter over the swingbridge at the harbour entrance. Over the next couple of miles we see warehouses bearing shipping company names famous throughout the world - Cunard, Ellerman, Pacific Steam Navigation, Blue Star, Blue Funnel, and many more.

'In the buff and varnished wood interior of the carriage, nasal Scouse accents mingle with strange tongues. On the stations, it is virtually certain that during the day staff have assisted foreign seamen, maybe using sign language. In the dock road a line of Coolies, in single file, are a strange sight against the shunting

engines and lorries. 'As the train dips down the switchback at Bramley-Moore, we see an L&Y Pug on the High Level Coal Railway and glimpse a wagon tipping its contents into the hold of a grimy collier. Huskisson, Brocklebank, Canada, Langton and Alexandra Docks reveal larger warehouses, taller cranes and bigger ships. At Gladstone Dock, great Cunard and Canadian Pacific liners are at rest. Finally, we clatter into Seaforth Sands station. A fresh breeze comes in from the Mersey estuary and sands stretch away towards Crosby and Southport, quite a contrast to the smoke and teeming activity back down the line.'

There were problems with the elevated structure even before World War II. Accumulated dirt had blocked many of the drains and muddy slime was rotting the deck plates. Heat and sulphurous fumes from dock engines below had corroded the underside of the decking and numerous cross girders. Moist salt air from the Mersey accelerated the decay. By 1954 the metalwork was becoming very difficult to maintain and it was estimated that £2 million was required to put matters right. Total closure seemed the only option, but the proposal led to several vigorous campaigns to save the railway.

These efforts were to no avail and at 10.03pm on Sunday 30th December 1956 the last Liverpool Overhead passenger trains left Seaforth and Dingle simultaneously. It had been a wet and dreary day, but people came from all over Britain to witness the end. The company was wound up a year later and demolition of the viaduct was completed in January 1959. Nevertheless, there are three tangible remainders of the line. Half way up a rock face overlooking the site of Brunswick yard is the proud portal of Dingle tunnel, complete with inscriptions. A more spectacular relic is the underground terminus itself, now a repair garage. Ironically, few people are aware that a former station on Liverpool's best loved railway still exists! Finally, coach No 3 is preserved at the Merseyside County Museum in William Brown Street.

MD&HB SHED ALLOCATION MAY 1955

Locos with the 'No' prefix were still in pre-war dark maroon livery, whilst those without it had received the post-war light green paintwork. The exception was 5 which was still in maroon.

IC	Inside cylinders
OC	Outside cylinders
F	Fireclass locomotive
DM	Diesel Mechanical

HORNBY DOCK SHED

No.1	Avonside 0-6-0ST	OC	1904 (stored)
5	Avonside 0-6-0ST	OC	1918
No.10	Avonside 0-6-0ST	OC	1910
No.12	Avonside 0-6-0ST	OC	1911 (stored)
13	Hunslet 0-6-0ST	IC	1940
No.19	Avonside 0-6-0ST	OC	1924
No.33	Hudswell 0-6-0ST	OC	1910

CANADA DOCK SHED

8	Hunslet 0-6-0ST	IC	1937
9	Hunslet 0-6-0ST	IC	1940
No.17	Avonside 0-6-0ST	OC	1912
No.21	Avonside 0-6-0ST	OC	1913
No.22	Avonside 0-6-0ST	OC	1916
29	Avonside 0-6-0ST	OC	1920

HUSKISSON DOCK SHED

No.4	Avonside 0-6-0ST	OC	1930
6	Hunslet 0-6-0ST	IC	1937
7	Avonside 0-6-0ST	OC	1907
11	Hunslet 0-6-0ST	IC	1940
No.24	Avonside 0-6-0ST	OC	1916
No.26	Avonside 0-6-0ST	OC	1918
No.28	Avonside 0-6-0ST	OC	1920
30	Hunslet 0-6-0ST	IC	1941
31	Hunslet 0-6-0ST	IC	1941

PRINCES DOCK SHED

27	Avonside 0-6-0ST	OC	1918
34	Hunslet 0-6-0DM		1951

PRINCES DOCK REPAIR SHED

No.3	Avonside 0-6-0ST	OC	1930 (outside)
No.20	Avonside 0-6-0ST	OC	1913 (ditto)
No.23	Avonside 0-6-0ST	OC	1916 (inside)
25	Avonside 0-6-0ST	OC	1918 (inside)
No.36	Avonside 0-6-0ST	OC	1902 (withdn)

In marked contrast to its elevated course past the docks, the Liverpool Overhead Railway terminated in a musty tunnel at Dingle. On 31st May 1952 a dozen passengers wait for a northbound train. Despite this subterranean location, plenty of water seems to be finding its way down to the island platform. Photograph R.B. Parr.

A Liverpool Overhead train about to cross the large girder bridge at Herculaneum before plunging into Dingle tunnel on 29th December 1956, the day before this unique British railway closed. Over fifty wagons can be seen in Brunswick goods yard, together with a 750hp diesel electric, one of three built by English Electric at Preston for the Jamaican Government Railway. Photograph J.A. Peden Collection.

Liverpool Overhead Railway rebuilt set 24-14-8 arrives at James Street station en route for Dingle, the train having just crossed the bowstring girder bridge over James Street itself. The Royal Liver Building is partly obscured by the Mersey road tunnel ventilation shaft. James Street station had been rebuilt following its destruction in an air raid on 2nd May 1941. Photograph J.A. Peden Collection.

BRUNSWICK DOCK SHED

No.2	Avonside	0-6-0ST	OC	1918
14	Hunslet	0-6-0ST	IC	1931
16	Avonside	0-6-0ST	OC	1912
32	Hunslet	0-6-0DM		1944
No.43	Barclay	0-6-0F	OC	1918*

NOTES:
(a) Barclay Fireless No.44 was destroyed in an air raid on 25th June 1941.
(b) Avonside locos No 3, 5, No.12, No. 20, No. 23 and No. 28 were scrapped by 1959. No.2, No.4, 7, No.10, 16, No.17, No.19, No.21, No.24, 25, 27 and 29 followed by 1964. No.1 went to Liverpool Museum and No.26 to a playground at Skelmersdale.
(c) Hunslet locos 6, 8, 9, 11, 13, 14, 30 and 31 were scrapped between 1961 and 1969.
(d) The last steam engine to be withdrawn was Barclay Fireless No.43 in 1969.
(e) New Hudswell Clarke 0-6-0 diesels were 35 - 38 (1959), 39 - 42 (1962) and 44 - 47 (1966).
*based at Dingle Oil Jetty

DEPARTURES FROM LIVERPOOL CENTRAL LOW LEVEL
4.00pm to 6.00pm, Monday to Friday, July 1960

4.00pm	West Kirby
4.05pm	Rock Ferry
4.10pm	New Brighton
4.15pm	Rock Ferry
4.20pm	West Kirby
4.25pm	Rock Ferry
4.30pm	New Brighton
4.35pm	Rock Ferry
4.38pm	West Kirby
4.42pm	New Brighton
4.45pm	Rock Ferry
4.48pm	West Kirby
4.52pm	New Brighton
4.54pm	Rock Ferry
4.58pm	West Kirby
5.00pm	Rock Ferry
5.02pm	New Brighton
5.05pm	Rock Ferry
5.08pm	West Kirby
5.10pm	Rock Ferry
5.13pm	New Brighton
5.15pm	Rock Ferry
5.18pm	West Kirby
5.20pm	Rock Ferry
5.23pm	New Brighton
5.25pm	Rock Ferry
5.28pm	West Kirby
5.33pm	New Brighton
5.35pm	Rock Ferry
5.38pm	West Kirby
5.43pm	New Brighton
5.45pm	Rock Ferry
5.48pm	West Kirby
5.50pm	Rock Ferry
5.53pm	New Brighton
5.55pm	Rock Ferry
5.58pm	West Kirby
6.00pm	Rock Ferry

All trains called at Birkenhead Hamilton Square, giving a 3 minute service from Liverpool.

On 18th June 1956, set 7-16-19 calls at James Street en route from Seaforth to Dingle. This 3-car train was unique in that the motor coaches were wide bodied, but the central trailer was of the original narrow design. The Royal Liver Building rears up in the left background, whilst the White Star Offices in red brick and Portland stone on the right had lost its entourage of gaunt warehouses in the blitz. Photograph W.A.C. Smith.

Pier Head station, just 300 yards north of James Street, was the largest on the Overhead. Seen on 18th June 1956, a Seaforth - Dingle service arrives there in a downpour. Set 15-12-16 was rebuilt at Seaforth Sands Works in 1947, the second train to be so treated. Photograph W.A.C. Smith.

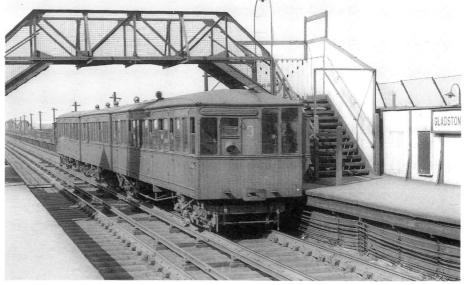

Gladstone Dock station opened on 16th June 1930 to serve the massive new port facilities nearby. A Seaforth - Dingle train (3-17-13, one of the original narrow bodied sets) arrives in the early 1950s. Car No 3 is preserved in Liverpool.

Top. Gladstone Dock station, looking south on 4th April 1958. Twin footbridges were necessary here to gain access to the southbound platform as the L&Y North Mersey goods station came right up to the structure on the landward side. Photograph J.A. Peden Collection.

Middle. Liverpool Overhead train 43-6-44 arriving at Seaforth Sands from Dingle on 18th June 1956. The cranes of Gladstone Dock rise up in the background. This station opened in 1905 on the new connection to L&Y metals, leaving the original terminus on the short spur to the right. Photograph W.A.C. Smith.

Bottom. Endpiece - or, maybe, showpiece. The original nameplate on Royal Scot 4-6-0 No.6130, carried from 1928 to 1935. The brass plaque had an engraving of the 0-4-0 locomotive LIVERPOOL built by Edward Bury of Liverpool for the Liverpool & Manchester Railway in 1831.217